398.20959 FOL

Folk stories of the Hmong

NOV    1992

**Wheaton Public Library**
225 N. Cross
Wheaton, Illinois   60187

GAYLORD

# FOLK STORIES
## of the
# HMONG

# FOLK STORIES
## of the
# HMONG

## Peoples of Laos, Thailand, and Vietnam

*Norma J. Livo*
Professor of Education
University of Colorado
Denver, Colorado

*Dia Cha*
Graduate Student
Northern Arizona University
Flagstaff, Arizona

1991
LIBRARIES UNLIMITED, INC.
Englewood, Colorado

LIBRARIES UNLIMITED, INC.
P.O. Box 3988
Englewood, CO 80155-3988

Interior book design and type selection by Judy Gay Matthews.

**Library of Congress Cataloging-in-Publication Data**

Folk stories of the Hmong : peoples of Laos, Thailand, and Vietnam /
  [compiled by] Norma J. Livo and Dia Cha.
    xii, 135p.  19x26 cm.
    Includes bibliographical references.
    ISBN 0-87287-854-6
    1. Hmong (South Asian people)--Folklore.  2. Tales--Asia,
  Southeastern.  3. Hmong (South Asian people)--Social life and
  customs.  I. Livo, Norma J., 1929-     . II. Cha, Dia, 1962-     .
  GR308.5.H67F65  1991
  398.2′089′95--dc20                                        91-370
                                                            CIP

To the Hmong people, who have taught me patience and appreciation for the joys I have.

*—NJL*

To Norma, whose hard work and enthusiasm have made this book possible.

*—DC*

# Contents

# Introduction

The Hmong people of Southeast Asia are some of the most recent immigrants to the United States. Like many ethnic peoples today, the Hmong are facing the rapid erosion of a once-proud and distinctive culture. Scattered from their home-land and decimated by war, they have been forced to migrate to whatever countries would accept them. Thousands of Hmong have settled in the United States and other urban societies, where the struggle for economic survival leaves them little time for studying or building on their rich cultural heritage.

The Hmong language did not acquire a written form until the 1950s. Therefore, the Hmong people have had to depend primarily on an oral and artistic tradition to pass on their history, legends, beliefs, and culture from one generation to the next. When the Hmong came to the United States, they brought their ancient culture with them as invisible luggage. Poetry, song and story, and hand arts, however, like every artistic activity, require not only mental ability but also security in the basic conditions of life. People who spend their strength working to ensure their own and their families' survival do not have the time or energy for artistic invention. Even traditional lore will eventually disappear if people do not have sufficient leisure time to cultivate it.

When asked why there are no Hmong artists in the United States, one elderly man explained, "The Hmong dream only at night. Artists need time to dream all day, too, and we have not had that time." In the United States, few Hmong adults are in a position to carry on the task of enlarging and transmitting their cultural inheritance, and Hmong children are busy adapting to American customs and ideas.

Co-author Dia Cha learned many traditional stories while sitting around the home fire of her native Hmong village in the highlands of Laos and listening to her grandmother, uncles, and aunts. Some years after the Vietnam War ended, the relocation of her family and many other Hmong to the United States affected their traditional ways; she realized the stories were being forgotten, the traditional art forms were not being pursued. Dia began to ask relatives and friends in the Hmong community to tell the stories they remembered so she could record them. She began recording the oral tales and the interpretations of the stories told on the *pa ndau* storycloths. Pa ndau (pronounced *pan-dow'*, sometimes spelled *paj ntaub*) are elaborate needlework pieces.

Interpretations of the oral stories and the stories depicted on the *pa ndau* were circulated through the Hmong community for discussion and clarification before the final versions were selected for this book. The stories featured here represent variations or combinations of variations on stories that have been told and retold among the Hmong, some for generations.

This book is an effort to collect and make available folk stories of the Hmong people, both to Americans who seek to understand the culture of their newest countrymen and to English-speaking Hmong children who might not otherwise have access to the stories and traditions of their people. It is only the beginning. Many more Hmong stories have yet to be explored and written down.

# List of Color Plates

# The Hmong and Their Culture

## History of the Hmong

Since 1976, approximately 100,000 Hmong have found their way to the United States from refugee camps along the Thai-Laotian border. This is not the first time that the Hmong people have found themselves surrounded by an alien culture. Many hundreds of years ago they migrated to Southeast Asia from their ancient homeland in Siberia and Central Asia. They lived among the Chinese for centuries, often as slaves, and were frequently targets of genocide because of their resistance to Chinese domination, oppression, and humiliation. In 1775, the Chinese, then consolidating the Manchu Empire, discouraged insurrection among the freedom-loving Hmong by displaying the severed heads of their leaders in baskets.

In time the Hmong settled in the mountainous terrain of Burma, Laos, Thailand, and Vietnam. The word *Hmong* means *human being* or *free people* in the Hmong language, and the people have always called themselves *Hmong* wherever they have lived. Never absorbed by the majority culture, they have been given different names by different peoples or tribes with whom they have come into contact—*Mang, Mong,* or *M'long* by neighboring tribes in Southeast Asia, *Meo* by the Thai and Laotians, *Meau* by the Germans.

The Chinese call the Hmong *Miao,* which the Hmong consider a derogatory term.* The first mention of the Hmong was in a Chinese text written 4,257 years ago. The Chinese wrote about the Hmong only during troubled times and often branded them as troublemakers. Before the Sung period (about 960-1280 A.D.), the Hmong who lived in the eastern region in Honan were referred to as Man, a name which also included the Yao people. The western Hmong were called Fan. Most scholars agree that the Hmong and Yao evolved from one ancestor in ancient times.

Bernatzik (1970) reports that the term *Miao* may have evolved from the sound made by cats. *Miao* is pronounced similarly to a Sino-Annamese written character meaning *cat,* and according to some interpretations of the Annamese

---

*See Diamond, Garrett, Quincy, Bernatzik, Pulleybland, and Yang in the bibliography at the end of the book.

1

language *Meau* means *cat*. Possibly the Hmong dialect reminded the Chinese of the mewing of cats, although an old Chinese historical work, *Mong-Tse*, compared the Hmong language with the cry or howling of the hyena. Another possibility is that the term refers to the catlike nimbleness of the Hmong, who are skilled mountain climbers.

Bernatzik also cites opinions that the term *Miao* arose from an agricultural context and that the ancient sinologists interpreted *Miau-tse* as *son of the soil*—from the Chinese character for *Miao*, which is composed of two parts, one meaning "plant" and the other meaning "field," plus *tse*, meaning "child." The Chinese may have used *Miao-tse* or *Miao* to designate non-Chinese foreigners as "tillers of the soil" or "the peasants." This implied that the *Miao-tse* were farmers who did not belong to the "great nation" of the Chinese, who used the term with a contemptuous undertone implying "boorish peasant" or "country bumpkin."

Despite their many migrations, the Hmong remained unaffected by international politics until 1959, when internal political strife following the French defeat at Dien Bien Phu led to the Laotian civil war. This and the war in Vietnam during the 1960s and 1970s resulted in the displacement of the Hmong from their adopted homelands. During the Vietnam War, the United States recruited the Hmong people and trained them as a tough fighting and intelligence-gathering force which operated against the Viet Cong. This force became known as the CIA's "secret army." In this role, the Hmong sabotaged war supplies moving along the Ho Chi Minh trail and rescued American pilots who had been downed over Laos. The Hmong participated in the toughest fighting and suffered enormous casualties. An old Laotian adage attests to their valor: "The Hmong are too tough to cry." But as one young educated Hmong said, "We know what fighting means—that the Hmong are the ones to die."

The Hmong continued to die after the war ended. When the Americans withdrew from Vietnam and Laos, the Hmong became the targets of genocide by the Pathet Lao. Many escaped to Thailand by crossing the Mekong River. Young men tell stories of how they tied their families together to pull them across the river. Babies were sedated so they would not cry and give their families away. Nevertheless, many were caught and killed. One man told of being halfway across the river, swimming and pulling his family, when he heard gunfire and looked back to see some of his family shot dead in the water. It has been estimated that over half of the Hmong population died during the Vietnam War and the subsequent flight to Thailand.

The fiercely independent Hmong have stood out because of their drive and energy, qualities that did not always endear them to other Southeast Asians. They remain incurable optimists. As Dr. Yang Dao said of his people, "We have made more progress in 14 years of war than we could have in 50 years of peace. Our economy has been destroyed, but the trouble has taught us what we can do."

2

# Traditional Beliefs and Customs

The Hmong still living in the highlands of southeast Asia probably continue to practice their traditional beliefs and customs. The many thousands of Hmong living in resettlement camps of Thailand, however, are unable to leave the camps and thus have limited opportunities to observe and practice customary rituals. Many Hmong have resettled from the camps into urban areas in the United States, further disrupting traditional habits and practices. Therefore many of the customs described here are no longer practiced, or exist only in a much-changed form.

Diversity is one of the most salient characteristics of the Hmong. For instance, different tribal groups may have different interpretations of ancient symbols, each group believing that its interpretation is the "real" one. The overall pattern of the beliefs, however, is common to all tribal groups.

Traditionally the Hmong are animistic. They believe that ponds, streams, rivers, hills, valleys, trees, rocks, and even wind currents all have individual spirits. Ancestors are particularly revered and are worshipped as though they possessed god-like qualities. Evil spirits live in areas not populated by people, and for this reason most Hmong prefer not to travel alone in uninhabited areas. Some Hmong believe there are spirits everywhere. Along the trail, for example, a trail spirit might cause a person to sprain an ankle. To placate the spirits of animals who had been killed, hunters in the Hmong homelands of Burma, Laos, Thailand, and Vietnam smeared blood on their crossbows after a kill. They also smeared sticks with blood and left them on the trail to warn others of trouble spots.

The Hmong also believe in spirit trees, on which they drape white cloths and strings. One Hmong family who had immigrated to the United States rejoiced at the sight of a tree that had been covered with toilet paper by pranksters. They thought it was a spirit tree.

Sickness results when evil spirits lure the soul from the body. If the soul fails to return, death results. Strings tied around the wrists, called *khi tes* ("tie hand") or *baci* (a Laotian word which means to bless or pray), symbolically confine protective spirits inside one's body. In the *baci* ceremony, blessings and good wishes are bestowed as the strings are tied. The Hmong adopted this practice only recently, probably during the 1960s. The Iroquois had a similar ceremony in which they tied leather strings around each other's wrists before storytelling in the belief that the strings would keep their spirits from leaving their bodies during storytelling.

The Hmong believe that several types of spirits commonly affect the mental health of individuals, including ancestor spirits, nature spirits, evil spirits, and house spirits. House spirits are generally friendly and help foster the well-being of the family. If offended, however, a house spirit may cause illness or mental health problems. For example, if a person curses when he bangs his head on the door, the spirit of the threshold may retaliate. A sacrificed dog, hind legs crossed, may be mounted over the door to placate the threshold spirits.

## Animal Symbols

Many animals are seen as having symbolic power. If a bird flies into a house and roosts, it is a warning or bad omen. If a snake enters the house, it is a sign that someone in the family will die soon. The woodpecker can pull worms and caterpillars from the growing bamboo spirit. Elephants are respected for their strength, and the Hmong avoid saying anything to hurt them lest elephants come and damage a family's property. Some say that elephants lead dead spirits to the otherworld. A particular black hoof on the elephant symbolizes whether the dead spirit is a mother, father, sister, or brother.

Souls of the dead may appear as butterflies. The rooster is the bird who awakens the sun at dawn. Toad lives on the moon and is connected to thunder. The crab covers the opening to the sky that permits the flood waters to flow. Many stories are told about monkeys. Tortoise brings advice from the spirit world and the ancestors to people on earth. Grasshoppers, according to a Hmong tale, were the first two living things on earth, but the sky spirit was dissatisfied because it thought the grasshoppers were stupid, so it created humans.

Other animals, like the bear, are feared. Tigers, which posed the greatest threat to small villages, were especially feared. In their native homelands the Hmong had no need for jails, because people who made trouble were simply run out of the village, and the roaming tigers took care of them. Spirits of people were sometimes thought to have been taken over by tigers. During the three days after interment of a dead person, the soul is believed to be unprotected. Evil spirits could drag the soul into the jungle, where it might be transformed into a man-eating tiger. If such a tiger were shot, the evil spirits took the soul with them. In time the soul turned into an evil spirit called a magic soul-tiger. A magic soul-tiger could be recognized because it had five toes instead of the four toes found on a real tiger.

## Farming

Rice has been the major Hmong crop for many generations. When a farmer chooses and marks off a site for a rice field, he waits for a sign to indicate whether the site is auspicious. If he sees either a barking deer or a wild pig jump up and run away, the farmer abandons the site and looks for another. If there are no bad omens, the farmer proceeds to clear the field, using the slash-and-burn method. When clearing a field, the farmer is careful not to talk loudly or laugh. If the first tree felled somersaults or if any of its branches stick into the mud, the spirits are telling the farmer that the tract is not acceptable.

When it is time to plant, the farmer digs a hole and plants a seed "for the birds." He digs a second hole and plants a seed "for the squirrels." A third hole is "for the dead," and the rest is "for the farmer." When farmers carry the rice harvest home, they are extremely careful not to let any rice fall into a river or stream because "If the Lord Dragon sees some of our rice drop into the water, he will think we have more rice than we need and make it decrease."

As the nutritive value of fields is depleted, the Hmong migrate to new areas. When a group of Hmong reach a new place, a scout tastes the soil; if it is sweet (because of the lime content), they know it will support crops.

The Hmong hold four sacrificial ceremonies each year in connection with growing crops. At each ceremony either a cow or a buffalo is killed. One ceremony is held before the land is cleared, the second before the seed is planted, the third when the crop is half grown, and the fourth after the harvest. These ceremonies are to call the ancestors and ask for their protection for the crop and later to thank them for their help.

## Houses

In native homelands, every Hmong house is built so that a distant mountain can be seen from either the front or the back door. Before building a home, the Hmong dig a hole a few inches in diameter and place as many grains of rice in it as there are people in the family. If the spirits move the grains during the night, another site must be found. Except in the lowlands, all houses are built on the ground with dirt floors and no windows. Many times a floor of bamboo strips is laid over the dirt for drainage. Each home contains a stove and an open fire pit with family bedrooms along one wall.

## Birth and Death

Moments after birth every Hmong baby receives a simple necklace, which warns the spirits that he or she is not a slave but belongs to a family. At birth, the child is automatically placed into its father's clan, which helps preserve the taboo against brother-sister marriage. Three days after birth, a welcoming ceremony is held and the baby is given a name. Hmong traditionally believe that touching a baby's head draws out the soul or spirit. If the spirit leaves the child, the child will get sick. It is also considered unwise to make a fuss over a child because this draws attention to it, and its spirit might be stolen as a result.

Hmong beliefs in life after death are very different from beliefs in Western culture. The Hmong believe that each person has three souls involved in rituals after death. The first soul is the one that normally stays with the body. The second is the soul that wanders; the wandering soul causes a person to dream while asleep. The third soul is the protective soul that tries to protect its owner from harm.

Upon death, the first soul stays with the body at the grave site. The wandering soul goes to live with the dead person's descendants. The third soul goes back to the spirit world and may be reborn. This third soul may be reincarnated as a

5

person, animal, or thing, depending on the person's past actions and luck. Therefore, both reincarnated souls and ancestor spirits remain around each family. Because of this belief, the Hmong always honor their dead ancestors during ceremonies.

The Hmong value the body in death as much as in life and believe that the proper treatment of a dead person's body affects his or her chances for reincarnation. Also, the fortunes of the living depend on the welfare of their ancestors. Therefore, it is in the interests of descendants to ensure that their parents and other ancestors have the best possible burial places. The deceased is dressed in an elaborate costume with a large collar having a pattern called the "dreaming maze" stitched on it; the care that is put into this stitchery reflects how highly the person was thought of in life. Whenever possible, Hmong are buried wearing special ornamental shoes. These are used to walk through the "land of the giant furry catterpillars on the way to the otherworld." The fingers of dead persons are often tied with red thread so that if they are detained in the afterlife by spirits wanting them to "help peel onions and garlic," they can say that their hands are injured and they cannot help.

## Chinese-Hmong Burial Story

Two brothers separately requested their respective descendants to bury them very close together, in the same ideal spot. The oldest brother was buried with gold beneath his head for a pillow. The younger brother had only a stone pillow. When the sons of the elder brother came to pay their respects at the grave three years later, they found that flowers—a sign of decay, which is necessary for reincarnation—had sprouted first on the grave of their uncle, the younger brother. They dug up the stone and gold pillows and exchanged them. The elder brother was thereby enabled to be reincarnated first, traveling along the lines of the dragon's veins to the pool that is the entrance to the otherworld before his younger brother. When the sons of the younger brother turned up and discovered what had happened, they realized how wicked their cousins were. "Since that time, we Hmong [symbolized by the younger brother and his sons] have never got on well together with the Chinese [symbolized by older brother and his sons]. We Hmong moved away and refused to speak the same language."

Similar themes occur often in the Hmong stories of the various reincarnations of Tswb Tchoj, the cultural hero who periodically arises to unify the clans and establish hegemony over the land. In these stories, the Hmong and the Chinese compete for the ideal site in which to bury their respective ancestors. Chinese deception and trickery usually cause the Hmong to end up with less desirable sites. Often the Chinese bury some form of metal in the Hmong graves. Because it does not putrefy, the metal prevents the decay that must take place in order for the Hmong souls to be reincarnated.* The stories also describe other ways in which the Chinese desecrate Hmong graves, just as the imperial dynasties desecrated the graves of other races. The imagery is clearly that of sovereignty and rebellion.

## The Shaman (*Tu-ua-neng*)

A shaman is a sort of combination medical doctor, psychologist, holy man, spiritual healer, and adviser. A shaman's services may be called upon when a person is sick, has mental problems, or is in need of spiritual or temporal advice. Often the shaman gives advice about ideal times to plant crops or to move a community, or about other activities of day-to-day living.

Most shamans are male, but women can also be shamans. To become a shaman, a person must be called by the shaman spirit. Physical training can enhance a shaman's ability to withstand the rigors of the trance state, which is necessary for entering the world of the unseen. The trance state is evoked by spirit helpers. While in a trance the shaman is believed to be riding his "dragon charger," his "speedy steed," or his "ship of wind and clouds." This fantastic Pegasus is represented by a bench on which the shaman rocks backwards and forwards as though riding a horse.

A shaman has two primary tools. The first is a veil that covers the head; use of the veil indicates that the shaman is absent from this side of reality and is blind to those who are present. The second is incense, which is burned on the altar. Other shaman tools include gongs, rattles, finger bells, and pieces of buffalo horn used in divination and in spirit healing. A knowledgeable shaman may use herbs and plants in the healing or restoring sessions.

During a healing session, the shaman has two main objectives. One is restoring the patient's self, which has a number of souls. Among them are the protruding shadow, the reindeer soul, the running bull, the chicken soul, and the growing bamboo soul. The shaman's mission is to find the errant soul and bring it back. If the soul wants to stay where it has gone, the shaman must convince it to return. By finding and bringing back the runaway soul, the shaman helps the patient to recover psychic balance and regain his or her health. At the completion of a healing session and bargaining for a patient's soul, a pig is sacrificed.

---

*The long historical record of struggle for control of material resources may explain why the Hmong regard metal as particularly unlucky. It was through knowledge of the principles of ironworking, around 600 B.C. during the mid-Chou period, that the early Chinese states began to establish their dominance over other peoples, including the Hmong.

When a shaman is near death, he summons his sons to his bedside and gives them the contents of his bowl of magic water to drink in hope of passing on the shamanistic spirit to his sons. The bowl is known as the "dragon pond" and is believed to be the place where the dragon who rules lightning and thunder comes to rest after having been invited by the shaman. After a shaman dies, his or her altar is dismantled and thrown into the jungle, but the shaman tools are kept.

## New Year's Festival

The New Year's festival is the high point of village life and is anticipated all year. In each village, the heads of clans, who are always the eldest men, meet to arrange the event. Each village plans its festival to take place at a different time, so that villages can invite one another to their activities.

The New Year's festival is often the beginning of intense courtships in which young people select and woo their mates. Wearing their finest embroidered clothes and silver jewelry, young men and women pair off and toss soft balls made of cloth back and forth to each other. Anyone who drops the ball must forfeit a gift (to be returned later) or sing a folksong. Later, the young man might visit the girl's house. He might whisper to her through the woven bamboo wall and play music on a small mouth harp. These activities begin a process of courtship that culminates with a raft of marriages following the New Year's celebration.

## Marriage Customs

In their traditional mountain homelands, Hmong girls who had attained puberty slept apart from the rest of the family so that young men would be able to visit during the night. Premarital sex, however, was closely controlled and discouraged by parents. A girl who became pregnant was considered a disgrace to her family.

Arranging a marriage was a matter of considerable maneuvering and bargaining. For this negotiation each family chose a spokesperson. A bride price, usually involving bars of silver, was agreed upon. The parents of the bride then held a feast of roasted pig in their home to celebrate the official announcement of marriage. This feast helped to bond the different clans. During the wedding feast, if the young man had abducted his bride without first negotiating with her family, his mother-in-law would accost him with a stick or oral insult. He would give her money (especially silver) as she tried to get her daughter back. No matter how she scolded or hit him, he continued to beg to show that he was serious and would be loyal to her daughter.

After the wedding ceremonies and banquet, the souls and good fortune of the young couple were symbolically wrapped up inside an umbrella that was tied with the band which had been wrapped around the turban of the bride. The umbrella was carried in a procession to the groom's house, where another banquet was held to welcome the bride and thank the negotiators, or *mej koob*. This was followed by the *baci* ceremony in which strings were tied around the wrists of the young couple and blessings and good wishes were bestowed on them.

Normally, as the bride entered the groom's house for the first time, a rooster was waved over her to symbolize that she was now a member of the groom's household. A new bride became fully identified with her husband's family. At one time the Hmong observed a levirate practice whereby a man's widow automatically became the wife of his younger brother. If a widow married someone other than her brother-in-law, the new husband was required to pay part of the bride price to the family of the first husband.

Divorce was possible but strongly discouraged. A woman who left her husband lost all rights to any of the couple's children that the husband's family wished to keep. The husband's family generally chose to keep all able-bodied males and any girls who could be expected to bring a good marriage price. In earlier times, the wife's family had to return the bride's price to the forsaken husband in the event of a divorce. In more recent times, the wife had to pay the husband what he had given for her.

# Hmong Folk Arts

## Jewelry

Several folk art examples of tribal traditions are found in Hmong jewelry. One of them is silverworking, which is usually done by the men. In their native homelands, a Hmong family's wealth was kept in silver bars, which were used for bride prices, trading, and commerce. For the Hmong, silver has a symbolic meaning as well as monetary importance.

A prominent piece in Hmong silverworking is a traditional necklace worn for special occasions. The necklaces contain lock-shaped pendants suspended by heavy chains from neck rings. Hmong folklore tells that, during the times when the Hmong were enslaved by the Chinese, slaves were forced to wear large circular locks around their necks for identification. After they won their independence, the Hmong designed the necklaces in remembrance of the hardships of slavery. Another explanation for the design of the necklaces is that the lock pendants are used in spirit-calling ceremonies to "lock" the wearer's soul into his or her body.

During the Vietnam War, the silver traditionally used for these necklaces became scarce. The Hmong then fashioned their necklaces using aluminum from downed planes.

## Clothing

Traditional Hmong clothing carries great symbolic meaning. Creation of stitchery and textile art takes time and skill. Hmong costumes and textiles are a statement about how women spend their time, the priorities of their culture, and the value attached to this art form. The cultural values of perseverance and hard work are exemplified in Hmong stitchery.

Each January, as men cleared the jungle by burning, women began a new round of sewing in anticipation of the next December, when the harvest would be celebrated at the New Year's festival. Because a person who wore old clothing at the festival was expected to have bad luck during the next year, it was important for every member of the family to have new clothes.

The quality of the needlework bestowed status on the women who created it. Young girls spent many years learning the sewing techniques and traditional designs necessary for the creation of Hmong clothing. At courting time, the beauty and intricacy of a girl's needlework invited admiration and assured her of a favored suitor. Some say that young girls who were skillful with the needle had higher wife value than those who were less skilled.

The finest needlework was done to commemorate birth and death. At death, the Hmong were buried in full finery. This gift of needlework consoled the living and ensured that the deceased would be recognized as being Hmong in the afterlife.

Babies are highly prized among the Hmong, and in some Hmong dialects the words for "flower" and "to be young" are the same. A birth is an occasion for making an elaborate baby-carrier, which is used to strap the baby close to the mother's back. These carriers are usually made of a rectangle about 23 inches long by 16 inches wide, with a smaller rectangle stitched across one end. The borders are usually made of several colors stitched together and accented with other hand embellishments. Sometimes bright yarn pompoms are added to the already color-ful carrier. Long bright sashes sewn to the carriers wrap around the mother's body to hold the baby securely in place, with the large rectangle supporting the baby's body and the small rectangle supporting its neck.

One article of apparel, the child's hat, reveals much about Hmong traditions and beliefs. The Hmong believe that without the protection of a hat, a child's spirit will escape through its head. The typical child's hat has a black fabric base shaped into a basic skullcap. This is covered with colorful embellishments of vary-ing types, including cross-stitches, appliqué, and sewn-on coins or beads. Sewn on the front of many children's hats is a vertical appendage that symbolizes a rooster. The rooster is considered a feisty protector, and therefore its presence on the hat adds protection for the child. Tassels, fringe, and yarn pompoms in vivid colors such as bright reds, oranges and yellows, hot pinks, and greens constitute the finishing touches. Some Hmong say that these colorful hats cause spirits look-ing down on a child from above to think it is a flower. Others believe that the hats encourage the flower spirits to descend and inhabit the child itself.

## Pa Ndau (Flower Cloth)

For centuries, it has been a tradition among Hmong hill tribes to celebrate births, marriages, or other significant events with gifts of squares of elaborate handstitching. When a person had accumulated enough of these squares, they were gathered together on larger pieces of *pa ndau*, with a border of triangles to scare away evil spirits, allowing good luck to come to the owner and his family.

Before 1965, *pa ndau* were used mainly to embellish Hmong clothing. Very thin needles, about one inch in length, were used for the stitching, which was usually done on cotton material. The dominant color was a deep indigo blue-black made from homegrown indigo dye sources. The accessibility of imported Indian and lowland Thai fabrics has greatly increased the range of color choices for Hmong needlework, and brighter shades of traditional colors now predominate. Some of the material used is a blend of cotton and polyester brought to the tribes from Bangkok. During war periods, parachute fabric was also used for the textile arts, along with fabric from GI sleeping-bags. Rice sacks and fabric remnants are still used as backing for the larger pieces of *pa ndau*. The backing is used to line the reverse side and to cover the stitches.

Contemporary Hmong needlework artists are not bound by traditional designs. Between 1965 and 1975, *pa ndau* artists began incorporating new designs in order to sell their work to foreigners. In 1975, the Hmong began migrating to Thailand and the United States and needed to find new ways to make a living, so they began creating new design forms and articles. The ever-resourceful Hmong now make a number of articles that would have no use in their own culture: pillowcases, embroideries and appliqués for skirts and purses, bedspreads, wall hangings, tablecloths, bookmarks, book bags, and eyeglass cases.

Hmong art acts as a bridge between the Hmong and American cultures. Present designs demonstrate the influence of American traditions. Many contemporary pieces use the colors of the American flag—red, white, and blue—a color combination not found prior to the Hmong's contact with Americans. Among current *pa ndau* designs are depictions of the nativity scene, Christmas trees, shamrocks, and American folk art quilt designs. Such innovations demonstrate the Hmong people's creativity and intelligence and show how they have adapted to a new life.

Many *pa ndau* designs also contain traditional, highly symbolic patterns. For example, the snail is a symbol of family growth and interrelatedness. The center of the coil of the snail's shell symbolizes the ancestors. The outer spirals are the successive generations, and the double snail shell represents the union of two families and also symbolizes the spinning motion used in many spiritual chants. Other animals are often depicted as well, such as the elephant, whose foot is a symbol of family wealth and power, and the centipede, which is known for its medicinal qualities and is highly respected. Tracks are considered the spirit imprint of the person or animal who has passed by; for example, tiger pawprints represent spirit imprints of tigers.

Triangles are used to represent teeth, fish scales, dragon scales, a fence, or a protective barrier to keep good spirits in and evil spirits out. The dream maze represents a pattern of right-angled appliqués; legend has it that a Hmong woman awoke from a dream to cut out this new and different pattern. A diamond in a square may represent the altar maintained in the home, the floor plan of a Buddhist pagoda, or the spirit imprint of the most powerful good spirit.

The snail-and-pumpkin-seed pattern is used on children's hats. Young souls tend to wander, and this pattern bonds a child's soul to its head until the soul is used to being in a new environment. A fish hook symbolizes a young girl's hope of finding a suitor. The eight-pointed star, which is sometimes referred to as the "left star," indicates good luck and is a protective symbol. The protective armor of the dragon represents the mythical dragon that lives forever, never knows sickness, and is respected by all.

Sometimes the Hmong deliberately insert a small area of a different color into a piece of needlework in order to let the spirit of the work escape. For example, a tree included in a much larger scene may have a tiny rectangle of different-colored thread worked into its trunk.

*Pa ndau* art incorporates appliqué, reverse appliqué, cross stitches, chain stitches, batik, and embroidery. Reverse appliqué involves combining three or four layers of different colored fabrics. The needleworker than cuts a design through the layers and stitches the patterns to reveal the several layers of fabric. This is a very intricate process and takes much longer to do than patchwork. Even the most skilled needleworker requires three to four months, or more than 600 hours, to create a large *pa ndau.* In terms of sales, Hmong refugees working on *pa ndau* make fifteen to thirty cents an hour. Nevertheless, some continue making the cloths in order to preserve their cultural arts and make a small income, although the art form is not as prevalent in this country as in their homelands.

## Storycloths

Hmong needlework represents a changing record of a people's history and culture and thus provides priceless information. Embroidered "storycloths" make direct reference to Hmong myths, personal family history, animals and village life, the death and disturbance of war and emigration, and life in a new land. Many storycloths originate in the resettlement camps of Thailand and are sent to relatives living in the United States.

The Vietnam War is stitched with accuracy by the Hmong women, who in unaccentuated but powerful ways depict the violence, torture, and death experienced by their people. The similarity of motifs indicates artificial influences and some standardization, but individual innovations are abundant, displaying exuberance, humor, and playfulness. Each artisan develops his or her own style from the basic designs. Because of the events of recent times and the inherent isolation of tribal groups, Hmong needlework is constantly changing. Their artistic originality allows a continual expansion of their art. No two pieces are exactly alike.

Sadly, this art form is rapidly disappearing and may already be an endangered folk art. Large works, especially, are increasingly difficult to find.

# Cultural Conflicts

The Hmong who have been uprooted from their homelands often experience prejudice and cultural conflicts in their new homes. In the Thai resettlement camps, for example, attempts were made to promote birth control among the Hmong, who have always valued large families. Instead of taking the birth control pills provided by camp officials, the Hmong ground them up and used them in their gardens as fertilizer.

Some medical treatments used in the United States are frightening to the Hmong. Operations are especially threatening because of rumors circulated in the resettlement camps that American people ate internal organs such as livers. Autopsies are also feared because they are believed to jeopardize reincarnation.

Another cultural conflict arises from the Hmong practice of coining—a coin about the size of a 50-cent piece is rubbed back and forth over the body to relieve muscle aches and tension. Coining results in what looks like bruises on the body, and Hmong have been charged with child abuse because of coining marks that have been mistaken for bruises.

In Laos, the Hmong men regularly hunted for food. In the United States, Hmong have gotten in trouble for snaring birds and animals in wildlife refuges. It is not easy to convey the concept of wildlife refuges to people who see wild animals as food.

The division of labor between the sexes has also undergone tremendous changes. Today, it is not uncommon for men in the Thailand resettlement camps to help the women in making *pa ndau*. What had been traditionally women's work is now one of the few opportunities for men to make money as well. Further, in the United States it is not unusual for Hmong women to find work as hotel maids or other jobs, while their husbands are left home to care for the children.

All of this adds to the stress of learning a new language and new lifestyles in a different culture, stress which carries tremendous costs. Many apparently healthy young Hmong men die suddenly and with no warning in their sleep. The medical diagnosis is that this sudden death syndrome is a result of stress. The Hmong are also feeling the loss of their traditional family structure. Many have complained about losing control of their children. What they considered to be discipline is now classified as child abuse. In all aspects of their lives, old ways are losing out to new beliefs and customs.

# Preserving a Cultural Heritage

The enduring power of the Hmong oral tradition continues to encapsulate and deal with changing conditions through the use of traditional folk symbols. But the younger generation of Hmong is busy learning to adapt to a new culture and has embraced education as a survival tool. These young people do not have time to learn folk art traditions. In Southeast Asia, every girl was taught to sew at an early age. In the United States, different skills are valued. Yet the loss of a people's cultural heritage is a high price to pay for adaptation to a new land.

Just a short time ago the Hmong believed that the world reached only as far as a man could walk. When an old chief in a northern Laos mountain jungle was asked how the Hmong had come from China, he said, "We were slaves. To escape we made a big cloth. Three thousand eight hundred Hmong stood on it. A good spirit made a big wind and blew us out of China into Laos."

In the late 1950s, messianic myths spread through the hills of Laos. One such myth prophesied that a prophet would come to the Hmong in a jeep, wearing American clothes, and handing out modern weapons. The transition from traveling on a giant wind-blown cloth to anticipating the arrival of a jeep-driving messiah symbolizes the transition the Hmong people are making from an old to a new way of life. Not long ago they carried on a centuries-old culture based on simple technologies and a family-based, tribal system. Today they find themselves in fast-paced, high-technology societies such as the United States, dealing with new concepts of family and work and a new system of values.

As has happened before in their long history, the Hmong are being forced to adapt to strange situations, aided only by their resilience, stubbornness, independence, and will to survive. Above all, the Hmong are survivors. They have not only salvaged and maintained much of their culture but have been generous in allowing other cultures to begin knowing them through their folk art and through stories such as those preserved here, stories that provide both unique and universal lessons which can be appreciated by all cultures.

# Color Plates

On the following sixteen pages, a number of native Hmong men, women, and children model clothing common in their former homelands. These Hmong are now residents of Denver, Colorado, and, for the most part, on a day-to-day basis, dress in a style more common to Western culture. Along with the native dress are color photographs of *pa ndau* story cloths and other *pa ndau* designs. Each plate is captioned, identifying the model and describing the native dress or the story depicted on the *pa ndau*. Accompanying the photographs are inked graphic representations of *pa ndau* and other Hmong artwork from *Hmong Textile Designs* by Anthony Chan with an introduction by Norma Livo (Stemmer House, 1990).

All photographs were taken by Michael Mancarella, design consultant to Libraries Unlimited, Inc., at Libraries Unlimited offices in Englewood, Colorado, during the summer of 1990.

Plate 1—This traditional headdress, modeled by See Thao, is of the White Hmong who live in the province of Sam Neua in northeastern Laos. It is typical everyday wear in the Hmong villages in this region.

Plate 2—This headdress is reserved mostly for festivals or special occasions. A portion of a traditional necklace is visible below Pa Thoa's collar.

17

Plate 3—Mrs. Wa Meng Cha dresses in a White Hmong outfit from the province of Xieng Khouang.

Plate 4—Mrs. Cher Tong Lee dresses in the costume of the White Hmong who live in Kham Kue Kham Moung in central Laos. Her necklace and others in these plates are made of silver.

Plate 5—This traditional outfit, worn by Mrs. Yang Thao, comes from the province of Luang Prabang.

Plate 6—Xia Cha wears a very contemporary Xieng Khouang outfit. His hat design is of the late 1980s. Prior to this, such a hat did not exist in the Hmong culture.

Plate 7—These costumes are common in the Kham Kue Kham Moung region of central Laos.

**Plate 8**—Mr. and Mrs. Ying Cha wear traditional outfits common to the Green Hmong from the province of Xieng Khouang in Laos.

**Plate 9**—Mrs. Wa Meng Cha (right) dresses in a White Hmong Xieng Khouang woman's outfit while Mrs. Ying Cha wears a Green Hmong Xieng Khouang woman's outfit.

**Plate 10**—In this picture, the four women dress in three different regional styles of Hmong outfits.

Plate 11—Yang Thao, See Thao (back row, left to right) and Yer, Hugh, and David Cha in outfits of the Sam Neua province.

Plate 12—These costumes represent four different regions.

21

**Plate 13**—Yer Cha wearing hat with rooster symbol-appendage.

**Plate 15**—This boy's outfit is Sam Neua, but his necklace is Xieng Khouang.

**Plate 14**—David and Hugh Cha wear boys' outfits typical in the province of Sam Neua. Their silver coin vests are reserved for festivals and special occasions.

Plate 16—Mrs. Ying Cha folds her costumes and stores them in her traditional *miaj loos*, a hand-woven basket of rattan.

Plate 17—Mrs. Cher Tong Lee holds a winnowing basket in her lap.

Plate 18—See and Yer Cha wear two different kinds of Hmong carrying baskets. The smaller basket is White Hmong and the larger basket is Green Hmong.

Plate 20—Mrs. Cher Tong Lee teaches her grandson to play a Hmong mouth harp, a musical instrument used in the courting ritual.

Plate 19—Young Hmong woman playing a Hmong flute.

**Plate 21**—*Pa ndau* illustrating Laos and its provinces in different colors and the different ethnic groups that reside in Laos. The Laotian flag is embroidered in the upper corners in red and white.

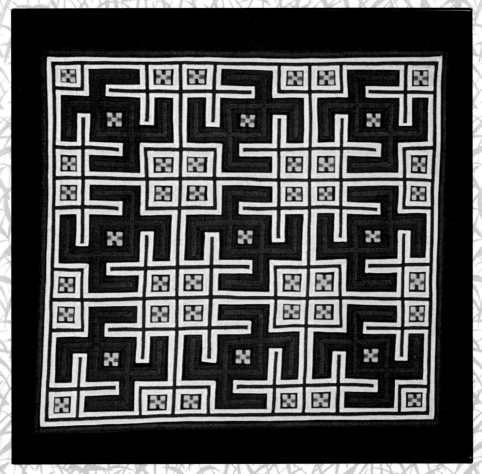

Plate 22—This pattern is known as the "old people's design" and represents one of the oldest and most traditional designs in the Hmong culture.

Plate 23—This *pa ndau* represents a more contemporary design responding to Western taste in color and size.

**Plate 24**—This *pa ndau* illustrates the story "A Bird Couple's Vow" on page 64.

**Plate 25**—Close-up of plate 24 showing the flame where the mother bird and her babies were burned in the field while the father bird, searching for food, was caught in a water lily overnight.

Plate 26—Close-up of plate 24. This scene shows the wedding feast of the king's youngest daughter (who was the mother bird) and the orphan boy (who was the father bird).

Plate 27—*Pa ndau* illustrating same story as plate 24.

Plate 28—Close-up of plate 27 showing fields, birds' nest, and fire consuming mother bird.

Plate 29—Close-up of plate 27. The mother bird reincarnated becomes the king's youngest daughter, but she is so angry she refuses to speak. The king and his family do everything they can to make her talk, until finally the king announces to the townspeople that whoever can make his daughter talk can marry her.

Plate 30—Hand embroidery showing different kinds of animals and trees of Hmong homelands.

Plate 31—Close-up of plate 30 showing the owl sitting on a tree branch and other animals scattered in the field.

Plate 32—Story cloth illustrates the story "The Tigers Steal Nou Plai's Wife, Ntxawm" on page 112.

Plate 33—Detail of story cloth illustrating "The Tigers Steal Nou Plai's Wife, Ntxawm."

Plate 34—Second half of story cloth (plate 32).

Plate 35—Hand embroidery in this *pa ndau* illustrates the natural environment, wild animals, and mystical creatures such as the dragons that have always been an essential part of the Hmong people's lives and culture.

Plate 36—Detail from plate 35.

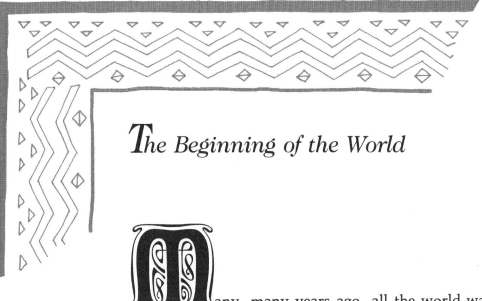

# The Beginning of the World

Many, many years ago, all the world was a rock and humans lived far under the ground with their animals.

As it so happened, one day a man and his wife were following their dog that was chasing a monkey through an endless rock tunnel. After a long trip they emerged on the surface of the world, a great black flat rock.

They returned home, gathered seeds and worms, and brought them to the surface. Soon the seeds sprang up, the worms multiplied, and life on the earth began.

# Legend of the Rice Seed

A poor widow, whose only child was a thirteen-year-old daughter, had to go daily to dig up wild tubers and yams near a large river in order to survive. One day the daughter disappeared and the distraught mother could not find her.

Later the mother was digging for food in the same area when she heard her daughter call out from the river. The daughter had married the Lord Dragon who lived in the river, and she invited her mother to come and visit her in the water.

After staying with them for a while, the mother longed to return home. The Lord Dragon gave her some magical rice seed specially packed in a leaf and a hollow reed, promising that if she planted it she would have more than enough to eat and drink.

The mother planted the seeds, and in time she had such a huge harvest of rice that she was unable to carry all of it home. She went to the river and asked the Lord Dragon what to do. "If there is too much rice," he replied, "stand in your field and whistle three times, then clap your hands three times."

The mother returned to her field and did as her son-in-law directed. Miraculously, the amount of rice diminished, and she carried home in one day all that was left.

To this day, her people continue to use a leaf and hollow reed for their ceremonial rice seed, and they never clap their hands or whistle while in a rice field.

# How Seeds Came Again into the World and Why Dogs Eat Feces Droppings

After the flood there was no farming because there were no seeds. So Dog, the only creature that could go to the land beyond the sky, was sent there to bring back seeds. The seeds stuck to Dog's furry coat, and it was easy for him to bring back corn, rice, and other field crop seeds.

As Dog was getting ready to return to the earthly world, the sky people said to him, "Oh, Dog. Earth people did not come to the sky themselves to get the seeds, they made you come instead. When you get back, you shall eat rice and the people shall eat feces."

"No," Dog replied. "I am carrying these seeds back for people to plant and cultivate. I will eat the feces droppings and let the humans eat the rice, corn, and other food crops."

Dog went back to earth, and there the people took the seeds he brought and they planted them. Later, they cultivated and harvested the crops. Dog did nothing.

The sky people came to Dog sometime after that, asking him, "Dog, what did you say to the earth people? Who did you say should eat feces— you or them?"

Dog answered, "When you sent me back, you told me to eat rice and for the humans to eat feces. But when I got back I told them that since they plant, cultivate, harvest, and also cook the rice, they should eat it. I would eat feces droppings and only whatever rice the people chose to give me."

So the sky people said, "Well, if that is what you want, that is what you will eat." This is the reason people eat rice, corn, and other grains and dogs eat feces droppings.

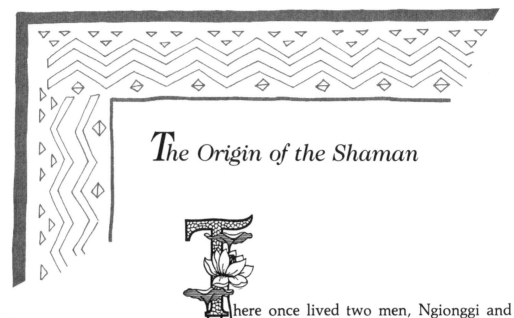

# The Origin of the Shaman

There once lived two men, Ngionggi and Xigi. One day, while at the seashore, they saw an island in the middle of the waves. On the island sat a crane on a nest with eggs. The crane left her nest for a time, so the two men took the eggs, pierced them, and emptied out their contents. Then they put the eggs back in the nest.

When the crane returned and saw that her eggs had holes in them, she filled them with a special substance. After forty days all the eggs hatched.

Ngionggi and Xigi saw what happened and they took some of the special substance because they thought that they could wake the dead with it. They tried it first on the corpses of an earthworm and an ant, and immediately the creatures came back to life.

The two men then went to a village where the chief had just died. They brought him back to life. The villagers, in gratitude, heaped presents on the two men. After that, the two men traveled everywhere raising the dead.

One day they decided to return to their own families. But unknown to the men, their wives and children had died long before. The bones were dry, and Ngionggi and Xigi were not able to revive them. Mad with grief, they threw their special medicine into a cave and decided that they, too, should die. Their countrymen tried to stop them from doing this but were not able to convince them. Ngionggi and Xigi consoled the people by saying, "After our death a spirit shall appear to some of you in your dreams. This spirit will make some of you shamans and teach you how to cure the sick. Consult these shamans when you are ill and you will be cured." Since that time, the Hmong have consulted their shamans whenever they get sick.

# Another Age of Happiness

In the beginning human beings were immortal and did not have to work. The earth produced everything people needed, and humans were free to travel between the sky and the earth. Life was easy and happy, with no problems or troubles.

One day, however, a woman drank from a forbidden stream and ate a forbidden white strawberry. Because of what the woman did, people had to leave their original homes and have never been allowed to return. Since then human beings have had to work, and they also became mortal.

For a long time people still lived to be very old, even eight hundred or nine hundred years old. But misfortunes and failures gradually shortened humans' lives.

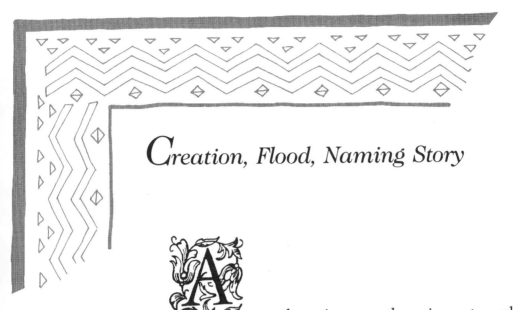

# Creation, Flood, Naming Story

A very long time ago, the universe turned upside down and the whole world was flooded with water. All living beings were killed except one boy and his sister, who had taken refuge in an unusually large wooden funeral drum.

The flood waters had risen higher and higher until they reached the sky. Then this drum bumped against the land of the sky and made a sound like NDOO NDONG! NDOO NDONG! Sky people heard the sound and said, "Why is the earthly world making this noise? What could be happening?"

Some sky people were sent down to find out what was happening, and they saw that the water had already covered the earth and reached up as high as the sky. The sky people said, "Let us use copper lances and iron spears to puncture holes in the earth so that the water can flow away."

So the sky people hurled the lances and spears into the earth and the water flowed down and away. Finally, the big drum came back down to the surface of the earth.

The brother and sister heard the noise when the drum came back to the earth, and they knew they had reached land. They broke open the drum and climbed out.

"Where are all the people?" the girl asked.

"Dead," said the boy.

"Are all the animals dead too?"

"Yes. There are only you and me."

They were both full of despair. "Marry me," said the boy. "We can have a baby. We can make more people."

"I cannot marry you. You are my brother," said the girl.

The next day the boy asked again, "Marry me."

The sister would not listen to him. But after many days of her brother asking her to marry him, she finally said, "If you really want to marry me, we must each bring a stone and climb up on that mountain. When we get to the top, we will roll your stone down one side of the mountain and roll mine down the other side. The next morning, if both stones have gone back up the mountain and we find them lying together on the mountain top, then I will agree to marry you. But if the stones do not go back up the mountain, you will stop asking me to marry you."

So they took two stones that were used for grinding and fit together smoothly, and each carried one stone up to the top of the mountain. The sister rolled her stone down one side and the brother rolled his stone down the other.

The boy wanted to marry his sister very much, so that night he went to the mountain. He carried his stone back up the mountain and put it on the grass. Then he went down the mountain again and carried his sister's stone back up.

In the morning the sister said it was too bad there was no one to come along as a witness. The two of them went to the top of the mountain. "Look at the stones," said the brother. "They have come back up the mountain and are together in the same place. Now we can be married."

So the sister finally agreed. After all, hadn't the stones come back up the mountain as a sign that it would be all right?

The sister and brother married and lived together as husband and wife. After a while, they had a baby, but it did not look like an ordinary baby. It was round like a big soft egg, and it had no arms and no legs. "What kind of baby is this?" they said to each other. "Maybe it is a baby seed. Let's cut it into pieces."

So they cut the baby seed into little pieces and scattered the pieces in all directions. Some pieces fell into the garden and made people. Their name was Vang, because Vang sounds like the Hmong word for garden.

Some pieces fell in the weeds and grass and made more people. Their name was Thao, because Thao sounds like the Hmong word for weeds and grass.

Some pieces fell in the goat house, and the people from those pieces were called Li. Other pieces fell in the pig house, and those people were named Moua, for the Hmong word for pig house.*

Three days later, the village was full of houses for every family. People were making fires and smoke was curling above every roof.

But this wonderful baby seed not only created people. Pieces also made chickens, pigs, oxen, buffaloes, horses, all sorts of insects, rodents, and birds. This is how the world was once more filled with living beings.

The brother and sister said, "Now we aren't sad because we are not alone any more."

---

*Vang, Thao, Li, and Moua are some of the Hmong clan names.

# 5 Why Monkey and Man Do Not Live Together

A long time ago, monkey and man lived together in friendship. But man was jealous of the monkey, because the monkey's field had lots of rice and the man's field was poor. But if you looked at the man's field from ground level it looked rich, and if you looked at the monkey's field from a nearby hill it looked poor. By showing the fields of rice to the monkey in this way, man tricked the monkey into changing fields.

Because his harvest was now so bad, the monkey had little to eat, so he went to the man to ask his advice. "You must kill your children," said the man, "so you will have more to eat." So the monkey went home and killed his children.

That night the man sneaked away from the village and gathered up the flesh of all the monkey's children. In the morning the monkey found the man getting ready to eat.

"What is that?" asked the monkey.

"Only bird intestines," replied the man.

But the monkey found out that the man had taken the flesh of the monkey's children, and he ran from the man and the village deep into the forest. Now the monkey steals the man's corn and rice because the man deceived him and stole the souls of his children.

# *Why Animals Cannot Talk*

In the early days, all animals, insects, birds, gnawing rodents, and creepy crawly worms and bugs could talk. But the master who ruled the world said, "This is not as it should be. If animals like caterpillars and ants are able to speak words, if chickens, pigs, cows, and buffaloes have language, if horses and all other animals can talk, then when a man wants to kill a pig to eat, there will be a dispute that will never be settled. If a man wants to kill an ox for meat, there will be endless objections and controversy. If a man wants to slaughter a buffalo for a feast, there will be legal battles and court cases without end."

Therefore, the master said, "Let only humans have language. Let all the animals—dogs, chickens, pigs, cattle, buffaloes—be dumb. Only people shall be able to speak. Then if a man wants to kill an animal, there will be no dispute, no protest, no litigation. Let humans raise livestock, because these animals are in the world for the benefit of people. If man only can talk there will be no troubles."

## 5 Why People Eat Three Meals a Day and Why Doodle Bugs Roll Balls of Dung

One day the sky people said to the doodle bug, "Go tell the people on earth that they must eat only one meal every three days. Do you understand? If earth people eat three meals a day, they will produce too much feces. Before long, the land will be so dug up and hollowed out by rhinoceros beetles [which favor fertilized soil] that it will not be any good for farming. It will be hard to produce food."

But the doodle bug came down to earth and told the earth people, "The sky people say you should eat three meals a day. That way you will have a lot of big bowel movements."

When the doodle bug flew back to the sky world he was asked, "What did you tell the earth people?"

The doodle bug answered, "I told the earth people that they should eat three meals a day."

"Oh, if you told them that, there will be too much excrement. Now you must fly back to earth and dig the ground forever, to cover up their feces. And your name shall be 'insect that rolls balls of excrement.' " And it is still that way today.

# 5 Why Farmers Have to Work So Hard

Long, long ago, plants and animals of all kinds were able to talk. They used words just like we do today. Here is what happened.

Lou Tou and his wife Ntsee Tyee were the first people of the Hmong. When they came to the surface of the earth from a crack in the rocks on a mountainside, Lou Tou carried a flower with him.

Each day Lou Tou and Ntsee Tyee ate a few seeds from the flower, until one day they saw that the seeds would soon be all gone. So they decided to plant the few remaining seeds.

After some time, a single stalk of corn grew where they had planted the seeds. But this was a special corn stalk, because on it grew several different kinds of grain. There were an ear of corn with seven leaves, an ear of yellow sticky corn, an ear of early white corn, a larger ear of late white corn, and three ears with three different kinds of millet. The last ear of corn on the stalk was white sticky corn, and the tassel at the very tip of the stalk was covered with rice.

All the grains on the special corn stalk grew and ripened. The first to ripen was the seven-leaf corn, and it returned to Lou Tou and Ntsee Tyee's house. "Mama and Papa, if you please, open the door," it said.

Lou Tou and Ntsee Tyee looked at each other. They did not recognize the voice, so they replied, "We would be willing to open the door, but you must tell us who you are."

"I am the seven-leaf ear of corn. I am part of the flower you brought with you from inside the earth."

"Where are you going to stay if we let you come in?" asked Lou Tou.

"Since I am small and don't want to be cold, I would like to be hung from the ceiling joists under the attic platform."

Shortly after that the yellow sticky corn ripened and came to the couple's door. "Mama and Papa, please open the door," it said.

"Yes, we will open the door, but who are you?" they asked.

The answer was, "We are part of the flower you brought from inside the earth."

"Where are you going to find room if we let you come in?" they asked again.

"We would like to hang under the attic floor, from the ceiling joists," answered the ears of yellow sticky corn. When the door was opened, they came in and were hung beside the ear of seven-leaf corn.

A few days later the early maturing corn asked to come into Lou Tou and Ntsee Tyee's house. "Who are you?" they asked the corn.

"We are part of the flower. We are the early corn," was the answer.

"Where do you want to be put?" the couple asked.

"Hang us under the attic floor," said the early corn. And so they were hung alongside the other corn.

Several days later, the late maturing corn came and said, "Mama and Papa, open the door for us."

"Who are you?" Lou Tou and his wife asked.

"We are part of the flower. We are the ears of late corn," came the reply.

"Where do you want to stay?" the couple asked.

"There are a lot of us. We want to stay in a special small room." So Lou Tou and Ntsee Tyee built a granary on tall poles, to keep the small room off the ground. That way the rats could not get to the room. There they stored the late maturing corn.

Shortly after they finished building the granary, the couple heard again, "Mama and Papa, please open the door."

"We will open the door, but who are you?"

"We are part of the flower. We are grains of millet. We have had a lot of trouble living and growing. Most of our grains died, but we have managed to come home," the millet said.

"Where do you want to stay?" asked the couple.

"We would like to stay in a basket up in the attic, right over the fireplace."

Lou Tou had to weave a basket to hold the millet. When he was finished, he put the millet in the basket in the attic.

A few days later, the grains of another kind of millet asked to come in. "Who are you?" asked Ntsee Tyee and Lou Tou.

"We are part of the flower. We are millet grains. Many of us had trouble growing and each cluster of us is only half filled out. We are ripe though. Please let us come back home."

"Where do you want to stay?" the couple asked the millet.

"We would like to stay in a large storage basket." And so a large bamboo storage bin was made ready to hold the grain.

Several days later, the grains of rice arrived and asked, "If you please, Mama and Papa, open the door."

"Who are you?" demanded Lou Tou and his wife.

"We are part of the flower. We are ripe and want to come back home," the rice said.

"Where do you want to stay?" the couple asked the rice.

"We would like to stay in a large, strong basket."

So Lou Tou had to weave another basket like the large storage bin for the grains of rice.

Lou Tou and Ntsee Tyee now had all kinds of grain. They had all they needed to plant and grow crops to eat. That was the way it was on earth for a long time: The grains always came to the home of the farmer when they were ripe and ready to use.

Many, many years later, a Hmong farmer went out one day to clear land to make a new field to plant grain. First he cut down the bamboo and trees. They cried and cried without stopping.

Then he cut away all of the plants already growing on the ground and set fire to them. The fire spread to the whole field and all the plants, trees, and bamboo sobbed and wailed. They cried without stopping.

The Hmong farmer planted the field in rice and corn. A short time after he planted the grains, they sprouted all together and began to grow. But oh! When the little plants were as big as the curved feathers in a rooster's tail, all the wild plants began to grow back, too. The wild plants began hitting the rice and corn and breaking them down.

"This will never do," said the corn and rice. So they went and told the farmer what was happening. "Mr. Hmong Farmer, you went out and planted us in the heart of the forest. Now the bamboo groves and trees that are growing there are banging into us and hitting us. They are breaking off our hands and our feet. Why did you plant us there? If you don't help us we won't survive."

The farmer told them, "Dear corn and rice, go and wait for seven days and I will come. In seven days I will come to where you live. I will make sure those wild plants won't hurt you anymore."

When the rice and corn got back to the forest field, they said to the wild plants and trees, "You better quit hitting and hurting us. We have a strong farmer who is going to come and see you. When he comes he will make trouble for you. There is no telling what he might do to you! We have told him all about you."

The bamboo, trees, and plants answered the grain, "If that is so, tell us what your farmer looks like."

"Our farmer is a man who wears a broad-brimmed, wool felt hat. His clothes are black and he carries a big knife. He will be puffing on a pipe. Just keep watching and when you see a man like that, he is the one," replied the grain.

The next day a tiger passed through the field. The bamboo, trees, vines, bushes, weeds, and grass started hitting the rice and corn and sneered, "Is this your owner?"

"No, it is not, no, it is not, no, it is not," chanted the rice and corn. "Not this one."

The very next day a bobcat sauntered by. While the bobcat passed, the wild plants began hitting the rice and corn again. "Is he the one?"

"No, he is not, no, he is not, no, he is not," came the reply. "Please, don't hit us like that! It hurts so much."

The third day a rat came scurrying through the field, pushing his way through the leaves and grass. The wild plants laughed and taunted, "Ha! Is this little creature with the long tail your chief? Your leader? Your owner?"

"No, he is not, no, he is not, no, he is not," whispered the rice and the corn.

"You are lucky, corn and rice, because if he is, we could just fall on him and crush him. He is so little we could easily take care of him!"

During the fourth day, a snorting bull came through the field. He was going to eat the grass plants, but the plants were rough and had stickers on them that hurt his mouth, so he went on. The wild plants asked, "Is this one your chief?"

"No, he is not, no, he is not, no, he is not," came the answer.

The fifth day a wolf went by. The wild plants asked, "Is this the one or not?"

"No, he is not the one either," groaned the rice and corn.

The sixth day a chicken flew over the field. "Ha, ha, ha! Is that your brave owner?" the wild plants taunted.

"No, he is not, no, he is not, no, he is not," was the reply.

At last the seventh day arrived. The Hmong farmer walked and walked and walked on his way to the field. He walked for half a day to get there. When he arrived the weeds and other harmful plants asked the corn and rice, "Is this your chief, your owner and protector?"

The rice and corn sighed with relief. "Yes, he is. He is the very one. Take a good look at him!"

The Hmong farmer began to chop the weeds and wild plants with his big knife. The wild plants all started crying at once, wailing and lamenting without end. The farmer sliced their necks so their heads fell off, PLOP! He cut them all off, all of the weeds in the whole field.

And so, at last the rice and corn grew and got big. The rice told the farmer, "Ah, Mr. Hmong Farmer, you have helped us very much, in many, many ways. Now you can go home and rest. You planted us and took care of us, and now you can stay home. We will come to you when we are ripe. But you have one more thing to do. Make a granary for us to live in at your home. We will come to you on our own when we are fully grown."

So the farmer went home. He did nothing, however, but went straight to bed. He lazed around in bed for a long time. In fact, he stayed in bed so long that his ear became flat and stuck to his head.

When the rice and corn were fully grown they all came at once, like a stream of flowing water, to the farmer's home. But there was no place ready for them to stay. There was no storage house, no bins, no granary, nothing! That meant they would have to stay outside, and they would get wet and rot when it rained. The rats would be able to get at them and eat them. So the rice and corn told the farmer, "We have come to you as we promised. You do not have a place ready for us to stay. Since this is true, we will go back to the field and whenever you get hungry for something to eat, you will have to come and get us. Hereafter, you will have to work to bring us in."

And so the rice and corn plants went back out to the field in the middle of the forest and stayed there until the farmer came to get them. That is why, even today, Hmong farmers have to walk long distances to the fields and carry their harvests on their backs.

# Why Birds Are Never Hungry

A long time ago, when the world was new, there were two brothers who went hunting. After the long day of walking through the jungle, they got lost. They were worried and could not remember which way to go to get back home to their parents. For many days, they wandered in the jungle. They did not have anything to eat and became very hungry.

One day the older brother decided that he had to go to find food and wood for the fire. The younger brother also wanted to go to gather water. After they discussed their plans, they each went their own way. They agreed to meet back at the clearing in the forest where they were camping when they had gathered the necessary things.

The younger brother went up and down everywhere through the jungle, but he could not find any water. Finally, he was so tired he sat down on a stone to think. He tried to face in a different direction, thinking he might find water that way. While he was thinking, a bluebird was jumping from one tree to another, singing, "I know where your parents are, I know where your parents are!"

The younger brother was surprised, because he wasn't sure what he was really hearing. He stared at the bluebird and tried to listen more carefully. He hoped the bluebird would sing to him and say those words again. He watched the bluebird wherever it went. After a time the bluebird started to sing again, saying the same words. The younger brother asked the bluebird, "Did you say you know where our parents are?"

"Yes, I did. But this is a bargain. If you can give me three insects then I will lead you to your parents," the bluebird chirped.

The boy paused a while and then he said, "Are you sure? If you are sure, will you also follow me now while I go to get my older brother?"

The bird agreed.

As the bargain had been set, the bluebird followed the younger boy to the clearing in the forest, where the older brother was sitting and waiting. He had been there for a long time  and had returned without either the food or the wood. The younger brother told the older brother about his bargain with the bluebird. Then the brothers left the bird in the clearing and went to find the insects. It took them quite some time, but they finally returned to the clearing and gave the insects to the bluebird.

After the bluebird had eaten the insects he said, "You boys must follow me wherever I fly and I will lead you to your parents."

The bluebird flew away, leading the two boys. They followed the bird closely, and after many days they finally got home. They were very happy, and they thanked the bluebird many times for leading them safely home.

Before the bluebird left the two brothers to go back to the forest, the boys told him, "We will never forget how you helped us. We hope that we can help you one day—to save your life, too. We will always give you food when you are hungry."

And that is why birds are always around people's houses now—because of the promise given to the bluebird by the two grateful brothers.

# Why Hmong Are Forbidden to Drink Mother's Milk

In the olden times, there lived a Hmong man who had seven wives. The chief wife was Hmong, the first secondary wife was Chinese, and the other secondary wives were all Hmong. Each of these wives gave birth to a son.

One day a very old lightning man with wrinkled eyes and a long white beard came, asking one Hmong woman after another to breastfeed him as they were doing for their babies. The Hmong women were very shy, so they wouldn't breastfeed the old man. But when he asked a Chinese and a Laotian woman to breastfeed him, they did. So he went back to the Hmong women and told them, "Because I am old you do not let me drink your milk. Therefore, from now on, after a Hmong person is weaned, they will be struck by lightning if they drink mother's milk. The Chinese and Loatian women fed me their milk. Therefore, the Chinese and Laotian people may eat and drink whatever they want to."

# Why the Hmong Live on Mountains

The very first king of the Hmong was a child who had remained in his mother's womb for three years. Because he was such a special child, he grew up to be king. He then lived in a palace of pure gold. One day, the Hmong and their neighbors had a dispute over ownership of land.

The king ordered both parties to depart at nightfall and to return before sunrise. He decreed that each would be the owner of the land they had traveled over during the night. The party that did not return on time would have to remain at the place where the rising sun caught them traveling.

At daybreak, the Hmong found themselves on a high mountain, and since that time the Hmong have lived on mountains.

# Shoa and His Fire

**S**hoa was a very wise man. He lived in peace with the animals around him as well as with everything else in his world. He and his friends—Wild Pig, White Bear, Tiger, Dragon, and Thunder—all lived together. Shoa had no problem talking with his friends, because he knew everything and could speak all languages. He could talk with animals and all the spirits of nature.

One day Tiger told his friends, "Maybe I should live somewhere else, because I need to make great noises and do uncontrolled things and if I do these things I will scare you."

All of his friends laughed at him and said, "Nothing you can do and no noises you can make will scare us. You are our friend, Tiger."

So Tiger told them to stay where they were. Then he traveled up to the top of the highest mountain, and there he snarled, growled, roared, screamed, and hissed. He dug his claws into the trees, tearing great strips of wood out of them. He jumped and bounced on the mountain top and shook the world below. When he came down off the mountain and back to his friends, he asked, "Were you scared? Did the noises and the shaking frighten you?"

They all laughed and said, "No, of course not. Little things like that aren't frightening."

Then Dragon said, "I need to live in a house of my own, because I am sure I will strike terror into your hearts when I get violent."

But Dragon's friends disagreed, so he, too, went to the mountain top, and there he made the sky turn black. He let water drop from the sky and then he dashed and threw water on the mountain. The water rushed and gathered speed. It tore rocks and mud from the mountain, washing everything down below until the river was muddy and full of waves. When he went back to his friend, he said, "I know that must have worried and frightened you."

But again, Dragon's friends smiled at him and said, "How silly! Of course a little thing like water didn't bother us."

Next, Bear said he wanted to have his own place to live in. "There will be times," he said, "when I will be sure to frighten you so much you will shake and quake, and I don't want that to happen."

They all assured him that he could never do such a thing. "Why, Bear, we are your friends. We know you. How could we ever be afraid of you?"

So Bear went to the mountain top and rampaged about, shredding logs. He stood on his hind legs, baring his teeth and claws and striking out at the wind and the sky. He threw his head skywards and snarled terrible snarls. When he came back down to his friends, he said, "There, I scared you, didn't I?" I am sure I did."

But they all said in a chorus, "No, indeed, old friend. You are magnificent, but certainly you didn't frighten or worry us."

Then Wild Pig did the best he could on top of the mountain, but again, no one was worried.

So Thunder said, "You haven't seen anything yet." He went up to the mountain top and made the sky churn till it was black and violent. Winds howled around the peak. He threw lightning from the black sky and broke trees and slashed long, deep cuts the whole length of the tallest of trees. He made noises that set the world jumping and he tossed lightning bolts in all directions. The whole world boomed and bounced with his power. When he felt sure his friends were frightened, he returned to them. "I am sorry I scared you," he apologized.

But they all laughed and said that he had done no such thing.

Quietly, wise old Shoa finally took his turn. He told his friends they had to build a house, so they gathered logs to make four walls, put thatch on the top for a roof, and pounded the earth smooth for a floor. Then Shoa told his friends to go inside the house, and he closed the only door. There were no windows, so they could not see anything he did outside. He gathered some dry grasses and twigs and put them in a pile. Then he struck a piece of flint against steel to make a spark. The *chink, chink, chink* noise it made wasn't very great. He asked them, "Does that noise scare you?"

They replied, "Of course not!"

So he did it again, *chink, chink, chink*, and with the sparks he set fire to the grass and twigs. He set the fire on the roof of the house. It blazed up and swept through the whole house with a whoosh. "Now are you afraid?" he asked.

For an answer he heard Wild Pig throwing himself against the door. Wherever the fire burned Wild Pig before he could get out, his hair turned yellow. Tiger bashed against the walls in the hot roaring fire, and wherever the fire touched him, his fur became striped. White Bear couldn't get out of the house before he was burned all over, and so his white fur turned black. Thunder flew off into the sky, followed quickly by Dragon.

The fire burned and burned without stopping for seven years. It burned the earth and the sky.

Today, you will never find Wild Pig, Tiger, Bear, Dragon, or Thunder living with the wise old man.

## The Story of the Owl

Long ago, the owl could see during the day as well as other animals could. One day, the owl was sitting by himself on the branch of a huge tree without much to do. He saw a monkey eating corn in the field and wanted to make fun of the monkey, so he suddenly made a very loud noise. "Hoot!" the owl cried.

The monkey was frightened and immediately ran away as fast as he could. As he ran, he accidentally stepped on the stem of the pumpkin vine, which caused the pumpkin to drop and roll very fast down the field until it hit a nat plant (sesame). The nat plant had very tiny seeds, and they all fell to the ground. In fact, some of the tiny seeds fell into a rooster's eyes, and the rooster was blinded.

The rooster ran aimlessly, pecking the ground, and unintentionally picked up a few ants from a group of worker ants. The other ants started rushing around and then dug into their anthill to hide themselves.

This caused the anthill to collapse, and it crushed and killed a mother chicken's two chicks. The mother chicken was very angry because, of course, she loved her babies very much.

The mother chicken decided to investigate what had killed her babies. She first started to question the anthill. "Why did you kill my babies?"

The anthill told her, "I was standing in my place and did not do anything wrong. But the ants started digging into me and I collapsed and fell down and squashed your chicks. I never meant to do it."

Then she went to the ants. "Why were you digging in the anthill? It fell down and killed my babies," she said.

"It was not our fault. We were busy working and the rooster pecked a few of our workers, so we dug into the anthill to hide ourselves. We did not want the rooster to catch us," snapped the ants.

So the hen went to the rooster and demanded, "Why did you peck the worker ants? They started to dig into the anthill to hide from you, and it collapsed on my two chicks and killed them!"

"I did not intend to peck the ants," the rooster answered. "I was on my way to look for food and some seeds suddenly fell into my eyes and blinded me. I could not see anything. I pecked around with my beak trying to figure out where I was and I accidentally pecked the ants."

The mother hen waddled straight to the nat plant to find out why its seeds had fallen down and into the eyes of the rooster. The nat plant told her, "I was holding all my seeds in place, but the pumpkin rolled down the hill and hit me. It hit me so hard I could not hold onto my seeds, so I lost them."

Now the mother hen half-flew and half-hopped to the pumpkin plant. "Why did you roll down the hill and hit the nat plant? It lost all of its seeds and some fell into the eyes of the rooster, so he pecked some worker ants who started digging at the anthill to hide from him. The anthill fell down and killed my two chicks!"

The bruised pumpkin plant answered, "I was hanging on my vine when the clumsy monkey stepped on my stem so I fell down. I rolled down the hill and hit the nat plant. I did not want to do it."

Clucking and squawking, the mother hen ran to the monkey to find out why he had stepped on the pumpkin vine. The monkey chattered, "It was the owl! He made a sudden loud noise and scared me. I was afraid that someone was going to shoot me, so I ran as fast as I could and mistakenly stepped on the stem of the pumpkin vine. I am sorry."

Furiously the hen went straight to the owl and demanded, "Why did you make the loud noise that scared the monkey and made him step on the pumpkin vine? The pumpkin fell off and rolled down the hill and hit the nat plant and made all of its tiny seeds fall. Some seeds fell into the rooster's eyes and blinded him, so he pecked some worker ants and the other ants dug into the anthill to hide from him. When they did that, the anthill collapsed and killed my two chicks. Why did you make that noise?"

The owl just stared at the mother hen with his eyes wide open. Finally, she angrily grabbed the owl's neck and twisted his head back and forth. "You are a wretch. From now on you will see only at night because you are not like the other animals."

And that is why the owl can see only at night and why he is able to turn his head all the way around.

# A *Bird Couple's Vow*

any, many New Year's festivals ago, there were a couple of birds who vowed to love each other for life and never to leave each other. They needed to build a nest and they ended up laying their eggs on the beard of a spirit man. One evening the male bird flew off to find food. He landed on a lotus flower and sucked the nectar from the flower for quite a while. But suddenly the sky became dark and the flower closed up, *whoomp*, with the bird inside. He couldn't get back to the nest that evening and had to spend the night inside the flower. When the male bird didn't return, the female bird thought that her husband had left her.

In the morning, when the sun came up and shone on the flower, the flower opened and the bird was able to fly back home. When he got there, his wife said to him, "Why were you out so long? Were you out talking with other girls?"

"No," said the male bird. "I didn't talk to anyone. I went to suck nectar from a water lily and, while I was sucking, it closed up and I couldn't get out."

The female bird didn't believe him. Being very clever, the male bird said, "I swear this is true. If it isn't true, may something bad happen to the spirit man." When the spirit man heard that he was quite angry, so he cut off the nest from his beard and threw it away in a valley of long, tall grass, the kind that was used to make thatch for roofing.

Shortly thereafter, the eggs hatched. Then one day the people came to the valley to burn the grass where the birds were living. As the fire burned closer and closer, the female bird said to the male, "Let me stay on top of the chicks and you stay on the bottom. Let both of us die with our chicks."

The male said, "No. Let me stay on top and you stay on the bottom." Finally the female let the male stay on the top. The fire burned up to their nest and then finally burned it, but the male flew away, letting the female die with the chicks. The female died, but she remembered that he had left her to die in the nest with their little chicks.

The female bird was reincarnated as a king's youngest daughter. She remembered her life as a bird, and she couldn't forget the things that her bird husband had done. In fact, it made her so mad that she couldn't speak.

After the male bird had flown away from his wife and chicks, he also died. He was reincarnated as a man.

One day the king proclaimed, "If anyone can make my daughter talk, I will let her marry that person."

Shortly after that, a young man heard about the king's promise. He went to the shoa (which means wise prophet in Hmong) and said, "Shoa, I want to marry the king's daughter. Please help me and tell me what I can say to this lady that would make her talk to me."

Shoa remembered the birds and said, "Don't you remember when fire burned the valley of the long, tall grass? You flew away and let her die with your chicks. You only need go to her and tell her what you did. But instead of saying that you flew away and left her and the chicks to die, you should say that the female flew away and the male died with the chicks. Then she will answer you, of course."

So the young man traveled to the king's palace. He said to the king's daughter, "Let me tell you a story. A long time ago, there were a couple of birds. They made a nest on the spirit man's beard. But the spirit man cut off their nest and threw it into the valley of the long, tall grass. When people burned the valley of grass, the male bird said that he should stay on top of the chicks and that both he and his wife would die with the chicks in the fire. The female disagreed, so the male let the female stay on top of the chicks and he stayed under them. But when the fire burned their nest, the female flew away and left the male to die with the chicks."

The girl spluttered and cried, "You are wrong! The male bird was on top!" The man answered, "No, the female was on top."

They kept arguing back and forth about which bird was on the top. The king heard them and said, "This young man has succeeded in getting my daughter to talk. I will keep my promise and let him marry her."

So they were married, and that is how the couple once again became husband and wife.

# The Monkeys and the Grasshoppers

One day a group of monkeys came upon the body of a dead monkey in the jungle. They could see that he had been killed, and the group decided it must have been the grasshoppers that killed their cousin. "We must fight them," said one of the monkeys.

They went to the grasshopper hill early the next morning. "Look out grasshoppers! We are going to fight you for killing our cousin," the monkeys cried.

"Oh, no!" said the grasshoppers. "You are wrong! We did not kill your cousin."

A loud, angry answer came back from the monkeys. "Yes, you did. You killed our cousin and you will pay for it!"

"Can we wait a little while to fight?" the grasshoppers pleaded. "It is so early in the morning and it is so cold. Can we wait until the sun comes up?"

The monkeys agreed to this, and so they waited. When the sun came up and warmed the grasshoppers, the fight began. The grasshoppers hopped on the monkeys' heads. All of the monkeys grabbed big sticks and tried to hit the grasshoppers, but the grasshoppers only jumped away. The monkeys instead ended up hitting each other hard on the head, *bonk, bonk, bonk!*

One monkey died because of this. Then a second monkey died, and a third, a fourth, and a fifth. After a while all of the monkeys were dead but one big monkey. He stood and looked around him at all of the dead monkeys, and he was puzzled. He decided to capture and eat the grasshoppers. He ate, and ate, and ate. In fact, he ate so many grasshoppers he finally died, too!

## Sister-in-Law Yer and the Tiger:
### How a Wise Woman Tricked the Tiger

Many years ago, when the corn still came to the people's homes when it was ripe, a young woman named Yer came to live with her sister and her sister's husband and their young children. Yer helped take care of the children since the family lived so far out in the forest, far away from the homes of their families.

One day Yer's brother-in-law went out hunting, and he heard a gibbon chattering loudly in the forest. He went to see why the animal was making such a fuss. He saw the gibbon in a tree but didn't see the tiger that was under the same tree. He shot the gibbon with his gun and the gibbon fell out of the tree onto the ground. As he was picking the gibbon up, the tiger pounced on him and ate him.

The tiger put on the man's clothes, picked up the man's gun, and slung the gibbon over his shoulder. The tiger said, "Now I am a man."

He headed for the man's home. Yer saw the tiger coming and said to her sister, "Here comes somebody. He is dressed like your husband, but he looks like a tiger." The wife looked and said, "Oh, yes, that is my husband all right."

But Yer insisted that it did not look like the man to her. She called out, "You are not my brother-in-law."

The tiger replied, "Oh, yes I am."

The wife gathered her three children and took them to bed. She said to Yer, "Good night," and got ready to sleep herself.

Yer decided to hide in the storage area upstairs. She fixed a bowl of hot red pepper, a bowl of salt, and a bowl of ashes from the fireplace. She took a blanket and climbed up in the attic. Yer put the three bowls on the storage platform near the ladder.

During the night she heard noises from downstrairs that sounded like *crunch, crunch.* Yer was frightened. She called down, "What are you eating that sounds like the breaking of bones?"

The tiger replied, "I am just chewing some stems of a hemp plant. Go to sleep."

But Yer had trouble sleeping. Just as dawn was breaking the next morning, the tiger said, "Sister Yer, it is morning. Come down."

Yer was worried, so she answered, "No, I won't come down. I think I will stay here."

"If you don't come down, I will come up," snarled the tiger, and he started to climb the ladder. Yer grabbed the bowl of salt and threw it into his eyes. The tiger screamed as the salt burned his eyes. Then Yer threw a handful of red pepper and ashes at his eyes, and the tiger frantically started to rub them with his forepaws. He fell to the floor and crawled to the door. "I am very thirsty, little sister. I am going to go down to the river for a drink." When he got out of the house he ran down to the river to wash his eyes. Yer heard him cry, "Oh, oh, oh!"

Yer quickly came down the ladder and gathered some food and more red pepper, salt, and ashes. Then she went back up to the attic.

Just as she put the pepper, salt, and ashes on the shelves, she heard the tiger return. "I am back from the river. Are you coming down now or not?"

"I am not coming down," Yer told him.

"Then I am coming up," threatened the tiger, and he started to climb the ladder again. Yer again threw a bowl of red pepper into his eyes, and a bowl of salt and the bowl of ashes. The tiger dropped to the floor, rubbing his eyes and writhing in pain. "Oh, oh, oh, oh!" Again he crawled to the door and ran to the river to wash his eyes.

Then a crow who often visited Yer flew to the top of the house. Yer told the bird to fly to her family. "Tell them a tiger ate my brother-in-law, my sister, and their children. Tell my family to come quickly."

The crow asked for something to eat. "Feed me and I will take the message to your parents."

Yer gave the crow some food, and after he ate it he flew off toward her family's home. The crow flew directly to Yer's father. "Yer sends word that a tiger has eaten all of the family except her. Now the tiger is trying to get her, too, and she begs you to come quickly."

All of Yer's family took their guns, spears, and sabers and hurried to save her.

Yer was still fighting the tiger off with the pepper, salt, and ashes. The tiger had made several more trips to the river. When Yer's family came, the tiger was at the river again, washing his swollen eyes.

Yer told her family what had happened. Her oldest brother instructed her to call to the tiger and tell him she would become his wife. Yer shouted toward the river, "Tiger, tiger. My family is here. They want to talk with you. I will be your wife. My parents and my brothers and sisters have come to give me to you."

"Aha, that's good. I will be right there." As the tiger said this he hurried to the house. When the tiger saw how many people were there he got quiet.

Yer's brothers began, "Oh, brave one, let's talk."

While Yer's oldest brother was talking with the tiger, several of Yer's other brothers went outside. They dug a hole in the path to the river, then covered it with some twigs and leaves. When they returned to the house, one of them said, "Dear tiger, your eyes look as if they hurt. Come to the river. Let us help you wash your poor eyes. We will help you."

Another brother said, "Poor future brother-in-law, your eyes are so swollen you must be having trouble seeing. Take an arm and the two of us will guide you to the river." The tiger walked between two of the brothers, but only the tiger was walking on the path. When he came to the hole covered by leaves, he fell in.

Yer's brothers then killed the tiger with their spears, and Yer's family took her home with them.

# Zeej Choj Kim, the Lazy Man

**A**long time ago, there was a man named Zeej Choj Kim. He lived with an emperor who had two sons and a daughter named Ntxawm. Zeej Choj Kim was very lazy, and spent most of his time sleeping.

The emperor's sons liked to go fishing a lot. Coming home from one of their fishing trips, they accidentally dropped a fish on the trail.

Zeej Choj Kim found this fish. Being very hungry, he picked the fish up to cook it for himself. The fish was quite dirty, so he decided to wash it before he cooked it. But Zeej Choj Kim was so lazy that he did not want to carry water from the stream to wash the fish. Instead, he washed the fish by urinating on it.

He cooked the fish in a fire pit. When the fish was almost ready to eat, Ntxawm, the emperor's daughter, and her family happened by and saw and smelled the fish cooking. She wanted to eat some of the fish. All of her relatives told her not to eat the fish, but she insisted.

After Ntxawm ate the fish, she became pregnant. Her father, the emperor, accused her of mating with Zeej Choj Kim, but she denied it. The emperor then went to Zeej Choj Kim and accused the lazy man of mating with his daughter. Of course, Zeej Choj Kim protested loud and long and said he was innocent.

The emperor did not quite know what to do about all of this. "If you two insist that you have not mated with each other, then I will have to wait until the baby is born. After that, we will take the child to look for his or her father."

When the baby was born, it was a sturdy boy. The emperor took the baby to every single man in town and gave each one the baby to hold. He decreed that if the baby did not cry, then that man must be the boy's father. But the baby always cried when each of the men held him. Finally, Zeej Choj Kim was told to hold the baby, and the baby did not cry, but smiled and gurgled happily.

The emperor was furious. He scolded his daughter. He raged. He told Ntxawm that she was no good. He asked, "Why did you mate with such a lazy man?"

In anger, he ordered his sons, "Take Zeej Choj Kim and Ntxawm to the river and kill them!"

The royal sons had no choice but to obey their father. As they walked to the river, one of the brothers said, "I do not want to kill Zeej Choj Kim. Remember when we built our house a few years ago and we asked all the people in town to come and help us quarry and carry stones? It took a lot of time, and even then we never had enough stones to build the house. But when Zeej Choj Kim chiseled the stones, he was so strong that the stones broke easily, just like dry corn. And the stones he carried in only one trip were more than enough for us to build the house. I suggest we do not kill him."

The other brother agreed. Instead, they walked Zeej Choj Kim and Ntxawm to the river and left them there.

The couple stayed at the riverside. They had no food and Zeej Choj Kim was so lazy that he did not want to go hunting. He just laid himself on the sand and did not move. He looked like he was dead. Two crows, one white and the other black, flew overhead and saw him. They thought he was dead, so the white crow flew down and landed on Zeej Choj Kim's stomach. The crow was just getting ready to eat him when Zeej Choj Kim

grabbed the crow's feet and yelled to Ntxawm, "I have caught a crow. We'll kill him and have dinner."

The white crow cried and begged to be set free, but Zeej Choj Kim insisted that he was too hungry to wait any longer. "You are dinner," he said to the crow.

The crow pleaded, "If you let me go, I will give you my magic ball."

"I want the ball first before I will let you go," replied Zeej Choj Kim.

The white crow called to the black crow, which was still flying overhead. "Go and bring my magic ball and give it to this man so he will set me free."

The black crow heard and flew away. But when the black crow came back, he asked, "White crow, should I bring the one that has one chamber or the one that has three chambers?"

"Bring the one that has one chamber and save the one with three chambers," was the reply.

"Oh, no," said Zeej Choj Kim. "If you bring the one with three chambers, then I will let you go. If not, I will kill you."

The white crow cried, "Black crow, bring the one that has three chambers."

In a little while the black crow returned again. "White crow, should I bring the one that has three chambers or the one with five chambers?" he asked.

The answer came, "Bring the one with three chambers and save the one with five chambers."

"Zeej Choj Kim demanded, "Oh, no! If you bring the one with five chambers I will set you free. Otherwise, I will eat you for dinner!"

"Bring the one with five chambers and save the one with three chambers," called the white crow.

*Folk Stories of Love, Magic, and Fun*

The black crow flew away. He came back shortly and asked again, "White crow, should I bring the one that has five chambers or the one with seven chambers?"

Quickly, the white crow replied, "Bring the one with five chambers and save the other one."

Zeej Choj Kim called to Ntxawm, "Begin to boil water. We will have to kill the crow to eat if he does not want to give us the magic ball with the seven chambers."

The white crow whined, "Don't start to boil the water yet. I will give you the one with seven chambers," and he instructed the black crow to hurry and bring it back.

Once more the black crow disappeared. When he came back he asked, "White crow, should I bring the one that has seven chambers or the one with nine?"

"Bring the one with seven and save the one with nine," said the white crow.

Zeej Choj Kim repeated what he had said before, so the white crow again changed his mind. "Bring the ball with nine chambers."

Finally, the black crow returned with the magic ball with nine chambers and gave it to Zeej Choj Kim. "Now that you have the magic ball, let me go," demanded the white crow.

"First, you must show me how it works. Then I will set you free," was the answer.

The white crow explained how to use the ball. "The first chamber is chicken. The second is pork, the third is beef, the fourth is vegetables, the fifth is rice, the sixth is mushrooms, the seventh is fruit, the eighth is water, and the ninth chamber is wine. When you want to eat or drink something you just say, "Daa daa chi fa, daw daw chi dhau." Then it will cook what you want."

"Tell it to cook some food for me before I let you go," demanded Zeej Choj Kim.

The white crow chanted, "Daa daa chi fa, daw daw chi dhau." A meal appeared. It was the most delicious food that Zeej Choj Kim and Ntxawm had ever eaten. Zeej Choj Kim let the white crow go. Now, they never had to worry about being hungry.

Meanwhile, the emperor was fighting a war. His soldiers fought for many days but they kept losing ground. One of the emperor's sons said, "Father, perhaps we should call our brother-in-law Zeej Choj Kim to come and help us."

The emperor roared, "I thought you killed him a long time ago. Did you not kill him when I ordered you to?"

"No, Father. We did not kill him," the son said softly.

"Well, I don't think he really could help us. Why even bother to call him—he is such a lazy man," mused the emperor.

The second son interrupted. "But, Father, it never hurts to call for help. If he can't help us then at least we can say we did our best."

Finally, after much argument, the emperor agreed. The sons ran down to the river to search for Zeej Choj Kim and Ntxawm. They found the couple and asked for help in the fight. Zeej Choj Kim agreed to help. "But first, you must go home and kill nine bulls and cook nine giant woks full of meat and bring nine giant hollowed-out wooden steamers of rice for me to eat. Then I will be ready to fight."

When the emperor saw his two sons return he asked, "So, will your strong brother-in-law help us?"

They told their father what Zeej Choj Kim had told them to do. The emperor laughed crazily and snorted, "I bet your brother-in-law won't be able to eat all that food. Neither will he help us fight."

The two sons ignored their father and did as Zeej Choj Kim had told them.

Finally, Zeej Choj Kim came. He had a bag with him. In the bag was the magic ball. After he arrived, he opened the bag and set the ball on the ground. Soldiers began to come out of the ball. There were hundreds and thousands of them. The first soldiers out of the ball ate and had already gone to fight when the next soldiers walked out of the ball. They, too, ate and then left to fight. Before the last group of soldiers had even finished eating, the first group had already won the battle.

When the emperor arrived at the battlefield, only three soldiers remained. He was very pleased and said, "Save those three to carry salt for us! My son-in-law, my real son-in-law, my amazing son-in-law, you have done a marvelous thing. Please come back with us and we will celebrate our victory."

Zeej Choj Kim and Ntxawm were invited to come back to live in town with the emperor and his sons. People paid respect to them, and they all lived happily ever after.

# Pumpkin Seed and the Snake

Once long ago, in another time and place, in a small village, there lived a widow and her two daughters. The older daughter was named Pumpkin Vine and the younger one was named Pumpkin Seed.

The family had a garden near the river. They had to work hard to prepare the field for the coming growing season. But they had a problem, because in the middle of the garden was a huge boulder. One day as she was working around the rock, the widow said to herself, "If someone could remove this rock from the middle of my garden I would let him marry one of my daughters."

At the end of the day, the family went home. The next day, the three women went back to work in the garden and found that the rock was gone! The widow started to laugh and said out loud, "I was only joking. I wouldn't allow either of my daughters to marry whoever removed that rock."

The widow thought that was the last of the giant rock. But the next day when the widow and her daughters went back to the field to work, there was the rock, in its original place in the middle of the garden.

Once more the widow said to herself, "If someone would take this rock from the middle of the field I would let him marry one of my daughters."

The next day the rock was gone again, but the widow said, "I did not mean it. I wouldn't allow either of my daughters to marry whoever removed that rock," as she laughed.

The next morning the rock was back in its spot, and the widow again promised one of her daughters in marriage to the person who could remove the rock.

Just like the other times, the rock disappeared from the field and the widow again teased, "I did not mean it. I wouldn't allow either of my daughters to marry the person who moved the rock."

The next morning the widow went to the field alone and found the rock back in its place. Giggling a little, the widow whispered, "If someone would take this rock from the middle of the field I would let him marry one of my daughters."

This time, a snake that was nearby said, "If you promise not to lie anymore I will remove the rock."

The widow was so startled that she promised not to lie anymore. The snake slithered from the edge of the garden, placed his tail around the rock, and threw it into the river. Since the widow's two daughters hadn't come to the field with her, the snake followed the widow home.

When they got home the widow called from outside to her daughters. She told them what had happened and said that one of them would have to marry the snake. Pumpkin Vine and Pumpkin Seed didn't want to marry the snake. They refused to open the door and let the snake into the house.

The snake and the widow waited and waited until it was dark, but the girls wouldn't open the door. Then the mother whispered through the door to her daughters, "I will kill the snake when he falls asleep." Even though her mother had said this would work, Pumpkin Vine, being the older one, still refused to open the door. It was very dark outside by this time.

Pumpkin Seed, on the other hand, thought that things would go as easily as her mother said, so she opened the door.

When the snake got into the house, Pumpkin Vine and Pumpkin Seed were frightened by its huge size and ugly shininess. Pumpkin Vine protested bitterly when her mother asked her to marry the snake.

The widow finally convinced Pumpkin Seed to marry the snake. The snake followed Pumpkin Seed wherever she went. It curled up beside her feet when she sat down. When she went to bed, the snake slid into her bed and coiled up beside her.

That night, with a sharp knife in one hand and a candle in the other, the widow crept into Pumpkin Seed's bedroom to kill the snake. But she discovered it was not an ugly snake sleeping beside Pumpkin Seed, but the most handsome young man that she had ever seen. She couldn't kill him.

The next day when Pumpkin Seed woke up the snake was still alive. She cried and demanded to know why her mother hadn't kept her promise and killed it. "I'll kill the snake tonight, Pumpkin Seed. Please trust me," begged the widow.

That night, the snake again slid into Pumpkin Seed's bed and coiled up beside her. The widow came into the room with her sharp knife and the candle and crept up to the bed to kill the snake. Again, though, instead of an ugly snake sleeping beside Pumpkin Seed, it was the handsome young man. Once more, she just couldn't kill him.

The next morning Pumpkin Seed woke up and there the snake was in her bed, still alive. She cried and cried and demanded to know why her mother hadn't killed it. "I'll kill the snake tonight, Pumpkin Seed. Please give me one more chance. Please trust me," pleaded the widow.

When the sun rose the next morning bright and warm, Pumpkin Seed woke up and there was the snake—still alive. Now Pumpkin Seed had no choice. She had to go with the snake to his home. On the way they came to a lovely clear stream. "Pumpkin Seed, I will go take a bath over behind the rocks. You wait here while I am gone." "All right," Pumpkin Seed agreed.

"When I am gone, you will see lots of colorful bubbles pouring down the stream. You must not touch the green bubbles. You can play with the white and yellow ones, but do not touch the green bubbles," warned the snake. Pumpkin Seed nodded in agreement.

The snake had been gone for a while when, sure enough, Pumpkin Seed noticed a variety of colored bubbles floating down the stream. She stood in delighted amazement as the bright, glittering bubbles traveled smoothly down the clear water. She eagerly pulled out some of the yellow bubbles. To her surprise the bubbles turned into gold jewels in her hands. Then she gathered some white bubbles, and they turned into silver jewels. Pumpkin Seed was so happy. She had never had such beautiful riches. She gaily put them on her neck, her wrists, her ears, and her fingers.

As she was admiring them she thought, "Why shouldn't I have some of the green bubbles?" So she reached down and scooped up some green bubbles, and before her startled eyes they turned into twisting snakes in her hands. They even stuck all over her hands. She frantically tried to remove the snakes, but they wouldn't come off.

A moment later a young, handsome man came toward her and she quickly hid her wriggling hands behind her back. "Why are you hiding your hands?" asked the man.

Her voice quivered as she told him, "Oh, my husband is a snake. He went up the stream to bathe and he told me to keep my hands like this."

The young man smiled and said, "I am your husband ..." Pumpkin Seed interrupted him. "No, you can't be!"

The man smiled and said, "Look at this!" He raised his arm and showed her the remaining snakeskin in his armpit. She believed him when she saw the skin and felt ashamed when she showed him her hands.

But he simply blew on her hands and the snakes fell off and disappeared like magic. Then they went home and lived happily for the rest of their lives.

# The Handsome Husband

**A** long, long time ago, there was a woman named Mua Nkau Tong who lived in a faraway place called Nuj Sua Teb Tom Taug. She was very pretty and she was famous for her wonderful sewing. In one day she could make nine exquisite pieces of *pa ndau* (needlework, or "flower cloth"). No other woman could sew that much, let alone create work of such beauty. But Mua Nkau Tong was not contented with her life. Within one year she had divorced nine husbands because she couldn't find the one right for her.

During this same time, there was a man named Tsi Nu Tong Sua who lived in another faraway place called Nuj Sua Teb Tom Peg, and he was incredibly handsome. But he, too, was not contented. In one year he had divorced nine wives.

Tsi Nu Tong Sua was also famous, because every year his harvest would fill nine giant *phawv* (storage silos). He was also famous for his ability to play the *keng*, a bamboo instrument. No one was able to match the beauty of his *keng* music.

Tsi Nu Tong Sua heard people telling the story of the beautiful, talented Mua Nkau Tong, and she heard tales about this incredible young man. As luck would have it, they both had the same wish at the same time in their hearts.

"I wish I knew where Tsi Nu Tong Sua lives. He must be the right person for me."

"I wish I knew where Mua Nkau Tong lives. She must be the very special person for me."

And so, on the same day, they both set out from opposite directions to find out the truth of the stories they had heard. They met each other on the trail about halfway. As Tsi Nu Tong Sua was walking, he saw a woman with the most delicate shining skin, with rosy cheeks and appealing dimples when she smiled. She was dressed in pretty shining clothes, carried a colorful umbrella, and walked with dainty grace. He would not take his eyes off her.

At the same time, Mua Nkau Tong saw Tsi Nu Tong Sua on the trail. He had his *keng* in his hands and was by far the most handsome man she had ever seen.

They turned to look at each other. Since they couldn't think of anything to say, they continued walking, and then Tsi Nu Tong Sua thought, "If I don't say something quickly, I'll miss my chance." They had already passed each other.

"Sister, where are you going?" he asked.

"Brother, I heard that there is a man named Tsi Nu Tong Sua who lives far away and who has divorced nine wives and built nine *phawv* in one year. I am on my way to find him. How about you? Where are you going?" Mua replied.

"I heard that there is a woman named Mua Nkau Tong who lives far away and who has divorced nine husbands and has the finest skin that glows, rosy cheeks, and dimples when she smiles. She can sew nine *pa ndau* a day, each more beautiful than any others ever seen."

Then they both exclaimed in unison, "That's me!"

They stopped and Mua Nkau Tong asked Tsi Nu Tong Sua if he would return with her to her home.

He told her, "That really isn't proper. You should go with me to my home." She quickly agreed.

They got married, but as they began their new life together, suddenly everything turned tragic. He became sick and couldn't farm. They called the shaman, and every time the shaman saw Tsi Nu Tong Sua he said, "What he really needs to do is go to study his clan's ceremonial and social customs." Tsi Nu Tong Sua didn't know these rituals, but the place for this study was quite far away from their home.

Finally, they decided that he must go and study. When he was ready to leave Mua Nkau Tong told him as she prepared his lunch, "Do not eat unless you are in a wholesome place. Do not rest until it is safe to do so. The time and place must be right to rest." She had had a premonition that Tsi Nu Tong Sua would be in danger. She knew that he was going far away where things would be different.

The trip took Tsi Nu Tong Sua through a forest area that he knew was not safe. It was enchanted, yet there was not another route—he had to pass through the forest. He knew this, so he agreed, "Yes, I will do as you say."

He left on the trip and traveled until he came to the forest. He started to walk through it. As he was walking he felt that he wanted to sing, so he did. He stopped after a while to rest. The sing-ing had made him forget the warning of Mua. Since he was hungry he ate. When he finished eating and drinking his water, he realized what he had done.

He was all alone in the forest and as he traveled he became thirsty. He came to a stream and noticed that people had crossed it. There were wet footprints on each side of the stream, and a leaf that had been used for drinking water was on a rock in the stream. He mused, "Some people have just passed by here."

As he was crossing the stream he suddenly felt lazy, and he used the same leaf to drink from. He hadn't walked ten yards when he saw Po Ntsong. This was the creature whose eyes were vertical instead of horizontal. Her feet were reversed, with the toes in back and the heel in front, and she had the ability to be either visible or become invisible.

Po Ntsong was lying on the path in Tsi Nu Tong Sua's way. He said, "Sister, will you please get out of my way? I want to pass." The vegetation was so tangled and thick beside the trail that he couldn't pass.

Po Ntsong said, "If you want, just step over me. I'm not going to get up!"

"Sister, will you please get out of my way? I want to pass," insisted Tsi Nu Tong Sua.

"If you want to, just step over me. I'm not going to get up!" she said again.

"Sister, I mean it. Please get out of my way. I want to pass," he repeated.

But she simply said again, "If you want to, just step over me. I'm not going to get up!"

So he started to step over her. Just then she raised her leg, and he fell down, trembling. He could not get up no matter how hard he tried. "Whoever can pull me up, I will marry her."

"Do you mean it?" Po Ntsong asked.

"Yes."

She took his hand and he was up.

"I was lying. I'm not going to marry you," said Tsi Nu Tong Sua. And he started down the trail.

Po Ntsong disappeared. She reappeared lying across the trail in front of him.

Three times Tsi Nu Tong Sua asked her to move so he could pass, but she refused. It was getting dark, and he was hungry and thirsty and still in the forest, so again, he started to step over her. He was crying and he knew he had to get out.

But Po Ntsong tripped him again. She fussed over him. She knew she had him. Since he was so very hungry and thirsty he had no choice, and he stayed with her.

Po Ntsong gave Tsi Nu Tong Sua a little branch of the tree with leaves and told him, "Hold it very still in front of your face with the shadow of the leaves covering your forehead, and I will go and look for food."

As he did what he was told, Po Ntsong went to a nearby village. She went to the house of the village chief. She turned herself invisible and stole rice and meat from the chief's house and returned with it to Tsi Nu Tong Sua.

Po Ntsong didn't eat human food. She ate worms, cow and horse dung, and raw crabs.

And so they lived for quite a while. Tsi Nu Tong Sua even learned to like Po Ntsong.

She had to steal food for him regularly, and he always held the branch very still in front of his face, with the shadow of the leaves covering his forehead. But one day Tsi Nu Tong Sua was sleepy, and the branch slipped to one side. Po Ntsong appeared at the village and as the branch slipped, the dogs saw her and chased her and killed her.

Tsi Nu Tong Sua waited until dark. When Po Ntsong didn't come back the next morning, he started to wander around, because he was quite hungry by now. He finally came close to the village and entered it. At the village's well the chief's youngest daughter, Ntxawm, was getting water. She saw Tsi Nu Tong Sua and noticed that he lurched as he walked. He was so weak from hunger that when he saw Ntxawm he begged for food. She ran back to her home with the bamboo water container unfilled.

Ntxawm told her parents and brothers about the man by the well. They all came out and led Tsi Nu Tong Sua to their house. They gave him a bath and food. Po Ntsong had cast a spell over Tsi Nu Tong Sua, so to overcome it Ntxawm's father put him in cow and buffalo dung. When Tsi Nu Tong Sua was himself again, he returned and married Ntxawm.

Ntxawm's family went out to the fields to farm every day while Ntxawm and Tsi Nu Tong Sua stayed home to feed the animals and cook.

One beautiful sunny day, while doing his chores, Tsi Nu Tong Sua wandered around the side of the house and started to think of Mua Nkau Tong. He said, "Where is my lovely wife on such a sunny day as this? Are you well, happy, sad, dead, alive? Dear wife, I didn't listen to your warning."

Ntxawm overheard this and became angry. She rushed to him, demanding, "What are you saying? I love you, my family loves you, and you still say you miss your wife!"

He tried to convince her that he was sorry until she forgave him and told him not to let it happen again.

Some time later, he was daydreaming and he said it again. "Where is my lovely wife on such a sunny day as this? Are you well, happy, sad, dead, alive? Dear wife, I didn't listen to your warning."

Ntxawm overheard him again and became so angry that she refused to forgive him. She was so upset she couldn't feed the animals, do the chores, or cook.

That evening when her parents came home from the fields, they saw hungry animals, work that was not done, and no meal ready for them. "What happened, daughter?"

"I am not going to work anymore. Tsi Nu Tong Sua says his wife is prettier than I am. He misses her and wonders how she is. I cannot forgive him," she wailed.

Her parents told her to cook dinner and then afterwards they would all sit down together and discuss the problem.

After dinner, Ntxawm told her story. The family decided that if Tsi Nu Tong Sua really missed his wife he should go back to her and tell her that if she wanted to keep him she would have to compete against Ntxawm to see which one was the prettiest. Ntxawm and her family would all go back to the home of Mua Nkau Tong. It was decided that after the competition Tsi Nu Tong Sua would then marry the prettiest one. The rules of the competition were decided. The families of Ntxawm and Tsi Nu Tong Sua would judge which wife was the prettiest. And so, the morning after these plans were made, Tsi Nu Tong Sua left to go to the home of Mua Nkau Tong. Three days later Ntxawm and her family would join him there.

When Tsi Nu Tong Sua got to his house, Mua Nkau Tong was working very hard. She had no help and she had to chase the sheep and the cows and do the farming and all of the chores. She worked so hard she didn't have time to even eat. She had become quite skinny since he last saw her.

Tsi Nu Tong Sua found Mua Nkau Tong working in the fields. He called to her and told her everything. He was very apologetic and contrite because he hadn't followed her warning. He told her about the proposed competition and the deal Ntxawm's family had made.

Mua Nkau Tong went back into the house and arranged the house and got her clothes ready. Early on the third day Mua Nkau Tong and Tsi Nu Tong Sua heard faraway music made with *keng* and drums. As the sun rose the sounds of the songs and music came closer. Ntxawm and her family had arrived. Ntxawm was dressed in many, many layers of clothes. The blouse reached up to her eyes, and she had so many skirts on that they reached up under her armpits.

When Mua Nkau Tong saw how Ntxawm was dressed she became very nervous, and she ran off to her bedroom.

After Ntxawm's family had settled in, they asked Tsi Nu Tong Sua, "Where is your wife?"

"She is in her bedroom," he told them.

"Now is the time. Ask her to come out," they replied.

He went in to Mua Nkau Tong's bedroom. "Are you ready? They want you to come out now."

Although she was fearful and nervous, Mua Nkau Tong quickly agreed. She wore a shining dress of gold and silver. She was very pretty. She looked as bright as a sword with the sun shining on it, gleaming so much that people couldn't even look at her. Not only were her clothes shining, but also her skin was sparkling. People looked at her from the front and the back and the side—no matter where they stood, she was beautiful.

Ntxawm's family said, "No wonder he misses her so much. There is no doubt or question that she is the most beautiful woman we have ever seen."

But Ntxawm refused to go when her family tried to get her to leave. She said, "No, no, no, no!" and wouldn't go. She argued that she didn't know that Tsi Nu Tong Sua was married to Mua Nkau Tong. All she knew was that he had been married to Po Ntsong and Po Ntsong was dead.

The families sat down to discuss the matter and finally decided that Tsi Nu Tong Sua should stand on the threshold of the doorway. Mua Nkau Tong would pull his arm from inside the house and Ntxawm would pull his other arm from outside the house. Whoever pulled him over the threshold would get him.

They all got ready. Since Ntxawm had been staying at home, feeding the animals and cooking, she was fat and strong. Mua Nkau Tong had worked so hard that she had become skinny and weak. As they pulled, Tsi Nu Tong Sua felt himself being pulled outside by Ntxawm. He saw that Ntxawm would win if he didn't help Mua Nkau Tong. He saw clearly that Mua Nkau Tong was the prettiest, so as she pulled his arm he helped a little. Finally Mua Nkau Tong got him inside the house.

Ntxawm was heartbroken and disappointed, and she cried. Her family led her back to her home, but after three days she died. Before she died, she sent a message to Tsi Nu Tong Sua that she wanted him to come back and be the only *keng* player at her funeral. The messenger arrived and gave the message to Tsi Nu Tong Sua. Mua Nkau Tong didn't want him to go, but the messenger begged and finally it was decided that Tsi Nu Tong Sua would go back with the messenger and stay for thirteen days. After the funeral he came back to Mua Nkau Tong. However, Ntxawm had captured his spirit at the funeral, so three months after he came back home, he died.

But Tsi Nu Tong Sua knew he was dying, so before he died he told Mua Nkau Tong that she should place his *keng* on his grave three days after he was buried, which she did.

Before Tsi Nu Tong Sua died, he and Mua Nkau Tong had a son. Now she had to take care of everything all alone. She cried as she worked and worked. Three years later, as she was watching the sheep from the hill, an old woman came by.

The old woman had all the characteristics of a good ogress and she knew magic. She saw Mua Nkau Tong crying and asked her, "Why are you crying?"

Mua Nkau Tong told her the long, sad story. "That's why I am crying."

"Don't cry, he is not dead. He is alive," whispered the old woman.

Mua Nkau Tong sobbed, "No, he is really dead. We buried him."

"If you really want to see him, I could take you to him," offered the old woman.

"Really?"

"Yes. If you come here very early tomorrow morning, I will take you to see him," the ogress promised.

Sure enough, the very next day the old woman came. Mua Nkau Tong put her head in the old woman's armpit and closed her eyes until the old woman told her to open them. They had traveled up to the sky world. People there lived just like people lived on earth.

The old woman walked Mua Nkau Tong down the street, and there they saw Tsi Nu Tong Sua, playing his *keng* beautifully. He was surrounded by beautiful women who were fawning over him. The women had touched his shoulders so much that the cloth of his shirt was threadbare.

When Mua Nkau Tong saw this she screamed, "What are you doing to my husband? Are you crazy?"

The women were embarrassed and quickly walked away. Mua Nkau Tong grabbed Tsi Nu Tong Sua's arm. "I thought you were dead! Here you are having a wonderful time, leaving me on earth to keep your house, your animals, your farm, and your son."

"How did you get here?" asked an amazed Tsi Nu Tong Sua.

But she ignored the question. She stuck to him, and wherever he went, she followed. Wherever he slept, she slept. He tried to persuade her to go back to earth. "Go back and watch over the sheep so they don't get caught in the rocks," he said.

Her answer was, "Who cares if they do? As long as I can stay with you I don't care."

He became silent. Later on, he tried again. "You should go back to clean the weeds out of the fields."

Again her answer was, "Who cares? As long as I can stay with you I don't care."

He realized she wouldn't return. "I have already died and you have not. We cannot live like this. Go back to earth, die, and then come back and we will live together forever."

And so, this is what she did. Her family buried her, and Mua Nkau Tong and Tsi Nu Tong Sua were reunited in the other world. They lived together forever with no more struggling. Since then, it is said that people will have a hard life on earth when they are so beautiful that they are wanted by both the spirit and earth people.

# Ngao Nao and Shee Na

A long time ago there was a family. The father had two wives and each wife had a daughter. The daughter of the first wife was named Ngao Nao.

The second wife had a daughter named Ngao Sang. The second wife became sick, so the family went to the shaman. He told the father, "The spirits of your dead parents want the sacrifice done. That is why your wife is sick." It is customary for a Hmong man to perform a cow sacrifice ceremony for his dead parents once in his lifetime. The man and his first wife went to find a cow for the ritual but, although they looked everywhere, they couldn't find one.

One day they came to a field of grass, where the husband hit his first wife with a rope three times and she turned into a cow. He led her back to their village and tied her near the edge of the village. He left her there eating grass. When he got home Ngao Nao asked, "Where is my mother?"

"She's coming, but she'll be late," was the reply.

Ngao Nao waited for a long time, but her mother didn't come. She asked the father again, "Where is my mother?" Again, he lied to her.

The daughter walked to the edge of the village and kept calling, "Mother, Mother, are you coming?"

The cow answered, "Maaaaa."

Ngao Nao told the cow, "Shut up! I'm calling for my mother, not you."

She started walking again, calling, "Mother, Mother, are you coming?"

The cow answered, "Maaaaaa."

Ngao Nao again told the cow, "Shut up! I'm calling for my mother, not you."

She went back to the house and told the father that she had called for her mother and the cow kept answering her. The father confessed what had happened. "The cow is your mother." Ngao Nao was sad and cried and cried because her mother was a cow.

Then Ngao Nao went back to her mother the cow. She cried because she didn't have a mother anymore. She told the cow how the second wife mistreated her and made her do hard work. When it got dark, she took her mother to the shed. The next day she took the cow back to the grass. She carried her loom in her basket to work with as the cow grazed.

The cow began to talk to her. "My dear Ngao Nao, put the yarn around my horns and I will help you weave." She did, and in a short while the cow finished weaving, so Ngao Nao took the yarn off and put new yarn on the cow's horns. By the end of the day, she had a basket full of woven cloth.

When Ngao Nao got home the second wife asked, "How were you able to get so much weaving done?"

Ngao Nao told her. The wife said, "Ahhhh. Then tomorrow my daughter Ngao Sang will take the cow out."

The next day Ngao Sang did take the cow out to the grass, and the cow did not like it at all. The cow led the girl into the nettles, which pricked and stung the girl. When Ngao Sang came back home with the cow she was quite sick from the pricks and stings and had no weaving at all. She told her mother what had happened during the day.

The mother and daughter both accused Ngao Nao of lying to them and scolded her. Ngao Nao cried for a long time. The second wife became very angry and demanded they kill the cow for the ceremony. The husband said, "It's not the right time. We have to wait until the time is right."

So the wife lied to her husband. "I have a headache, a backache, and a stomachache. Go and ask the shoa who lives in the hollow tree what will help me." The husband left to find the shoa and get his advice on what was making his wife so sick. Then the wife quickly put on some different clothes, went to the shoa's place, and pretended that she was the shoa. She got inside the hollow log.

When the husband got there he asked the shoa, "My wife is very sick. What is making her sick?"

The wife, pretending to be the shoa, said, "As the wise shaman of this village, I tell you that you must go home and kill your cow. After that is done, your wife will feel much better."

The husband returned home. The second wife took a shortcut and got home first, where she pretended to be asleep in bed. When the husband came into the room, she acted as if she were just waking up. "What did the shoa say?" she asked.

He told her that he was going to have to kill the cow to help her get well. She was quite happy at this, but the husband still felt it wasn't the right time for the ceremony. The second wife pretended to be even sicker. She wouldn't eat or drink. She asked him to go see the shoa who lived in the rock. After the husband left to visit the shoa in the rock, she again got up, changed her clothes, and ran quickly to the rock.

When the husband came and asked the shoa what he should do, she again pretended to be the shoa. "You must make a sacrifice of a cow. That is the only thing that will help your wife."

The husband returned home and the wife again beat him there by taking a shortcut. This time he began to think seriously that maybe he had to kill the cow. He called his relatives to a meeting to plan the upcoming ceremony. That night he was talking with his cousins. "Tomorrow morning I will kill my cow for my wife to eat. She is sick and the shaman says that will help her get well."

Ngao Nao heard this and was desperate. She went out to the cow in her pen and told her, "Mother, they are going to kill you. What am I to do?" The cow told her, "Ngao Nao, there is nothing we can do. But I am very afraid of the hammer. Go back and sharpen the knife. Stick it in the ground on the trail that leads to where they will butcher me. I'll fall on the knife and die. You must not eat my meat. Also, get all of my fingernails and toenails and my tail and put them in my food trough."

So Ngao Nao did as she was told. She sharpened the blade on the knife until it could cut silk threads and stuck it in the ground along the trail. As the husband and the family walked in a procession leading the cow, the cow fell on the knife and died. Ngao Nao gathered the nails and the tail and put them in the cow's food trough as she had promised.

The cow meat was cooked and a big feast was made ready, but Ngao Nao couldn't eat anything. Instead, she put the beef in the trough the cow used to eat from. She was crying all the time she did this.

The second wife and her daughter went to take part in the Hmong New Year celebration. The wife made many new clothes for her own daughter, but Ngao Nao had no new clothes at all. The wife told Ngao Nao that before she could go to the New Year's festival she had to sort the rice grain from the chaff. If she didn't get this done, she couldn't go. Ngao Nao was lonely as she worked, and she talked to herself. "Everyone else has a mother. Everyone has fine new clothes for the new year. They are all enjoying playing ball at the festival, but I am an orphan girl with no clothes to wear and am not even allowed to go to the festival." She remembered her mother and went to the trough and found it was full of shiny silk clothes. She put these on and went to the festival.

At the festival, a handsome young man named Shee Na played the *keng* (a bamboo instrument) so expertly and he even danced as he played. All the young girls liked him but he didn't care about any of them. Wherever he went three layers of girls followed him. While he danced and played, he spat. The second wife saw this and she told her daughter, Ngao Sang, to kiss the spit wherever it fell. When Shee Na saw Ngao Nao, he liked her very much. He thought she was the prettiest girl he had ever seen. Shee Na asked Ngao Nao to play ball with him. He followed her wherever she went, and wherever he went the wife and her daughter followed him.

Shee Na followed Ngao Nao home, along with the wife and her daughter. At dinner that night, the wife wanted Shee Na to marry her daughter so she seated Ngao Nao in a corner and placed Shee Na next to her daughter. She served rice and meat without bones to the couple and corn and bones with little meat to Ngao Nao. Shee Na said, "I'm very shy. If you won't turn out the light, I won't be able to eat." Of course, the mother turned the light out. Shee Na exchanged food from the daughter to Ngao Nao. Ngao Sang complained about the bones and corn.

"Don't lie, daughter. I gave you the meat and rice," said her mother. Things got quiet and then Ngao Sang started to complain again. "If you insist, I will turn on the light and show you," said her mother. Shee Na quickly exchanged the food again before the lights were lit. Ngao Sang's mother scolded her for being a liar.

Shee Na asked again to have the lights out so he could eat. They were turned out and he quickly exchanged the food again. Ngao Sang complained, "It is not nice to eat corn and bones. I don't like it."

Her mother told her, "I gave you the rice and meat. We did this once before. I'll light the lights again to show you." Quickly Shee Na exchanged the food, and when the lights came on the mother scolded her daughter again for being a liar.

All of this happened one more time. Then it was time to get ready for bed. The mother put Shee Na and her daughter together and the mother and Ngao Nao went to a separate place. When the lights were turned out, Shee Na quickly swapped the girls. He pulled the covers up so the mother wouldn't know if she came to check. The mother decided to put sticky beeswax on Ngao Nao's eyes so she wouldn't be able to open her eyes in the morning.

The next morning the mother got up early to fix breakfast for her daughter and Shee Na to eat before they left to get married. It was so early that it was still dark and she thought the girl with Shee Na was her

daughter. The mother even packed a lunch for them. They left and the sun rose high. The mother was sewing *pa ndau* and talking to herself. "The sun is shining. By now my Ngao Sang and Shee Na probably have traveled quite a way."

Then she heard the voice of Ngao Sang. "Mother, I am here."

The mother said, "Shut up, orphan girl. I'm not talking to you." She continued to sew.

The voice said again, "Mother, I am here."

"Be still, foolish girl. I am not talking to you," said the mother. And she continued to sew.

Yet a third time she heard, "Mother, I am here."

This time the mother became very angry. "Let me see you," she ordered. The mother warmed the girl's eyes with her hand and the beeswax came off. There was Ngao Sang! "I thought you were the one who left with Shee Na," she angrily said. The mother quickly fed Ngao Sang, packed her a lunch, and sent her off to catch up with the couple.

Ngao Sang followed them. But by the time she found them, Ngao Nao and Shee Na were the parents of a son named Tou Zong Kou. Ngao Sang decided to trick the couple. "Ngao Nao, since you married and left home, I miss you very much. Let's go and play and talk like old times."

The two girls went for a walk in the forest. When they were deep in the forest, Ngao Sang killed Ngao Nao with a knife. Then she returned to Shee Na's house. "Where is Ngao Nao?" he asked. "Where is Tou Zong Kou's mother?"

"I am his mother," said Ngao Sang.

"No, you are not. You are Ngao Sang. Tou Zong Kou's mother is the beautiful Ngao Nao." Shee Na sent a magical object to go where Ngao Nao fetched water, but she wasn't there. He sent the magical object to go where she gathered vegetables for the pigs, but she was not there. He sent the magical object to where she collected firewood, but she was not there. Shee Na knew something was very wrong, so he went to the forest and there he found his dead wife and buried her. He buried her with the ring on her finger.

He was sad for a long, long time. During all this time Ngao Sang took care of him and comforted him. She refused to go away. Ngao Sang kept saying they should get married. Shee Na said, "My wife had long thick hair she used for my pillow. You don't have hair like hers. How could you be my wife?"

One day the son went out to play and met a young woman sitting on the front porch of a house. They talked. "Where are you going, little boy?" she asked him. He told her that he was playing. The woman combed his hair. "Who is your mother?" she asked.

"She is dead," he told her. He felt rain drops on his head, but it was a sunny day. "How come it is a blue sky and I feel rain?"

"When rainbows appear that happens," she told him. They continued to visit for many days.

One day Shee Na asked the boy where he was going. Who was he playing with? Little Tou Zong Kou told him all about the nice woman with beautiful long hair. "She combs my hair and we talk," he told his father.

"Take me to see her," Shee Na said. They went together, and when Shee Na saw the woman he saw the ring on her finger. He wanted to marry her again. She told him that he must ask her mother. He must go to the old woman in the house and get her permission for them to marry. He followed her directions and the old woman gave them her blessing.

Ngao Sang was angry when she saw the couple. Later, when Ngao Sang was talking with Ngao Nao, Ngao Sang asked, "Why is your hair so long? It is much longer than mine." Ngao Nao got an idea. "It is because I boil the water in a huge wok until it is hot, hot, hot and then I put my hair in it."

Ngao Sang wanted long hair, too. "Help me get long hair," Ngao Sang asked. Ngao Nao heated the wok of water over a big fire. "Is it ready now?" asked Ngao Sang.

"Yes," replied Ngao Nao. Ngao Sang put her hair in the boiling water. As she bent her head, Ngao Nao pushed her into the water, and Ngao Sang died.

Ngao Sang's mother later came for a visit and asked, "Where is my daughter?" Ngao Nao replied, "Ngao Sang is very sick. She is in the room making those noises." Shee Na had put an old sow in the room and that was what the mother heard.

Without asking to see her sick daughter, Ngao Sang's mother left to go home. Shee Na put Ngao Sang's breasts in her basket. Later on the trail, when the mother stopped and put the basket down, she saw the breasts. She was furious and wanted revenge. She wished they were both dead. She wished so hard that her wishes came true. Shee Na changed into a tree and Ngao Nao became a beehive. Their son turned into a bird.

Now, whenever the bird comes, the bees have to leave the beehive so the bird can get a drink. They know that the beehive was the bird's mother.

# The Tiger Steals Nkauj Ncoom

Long ago when the world was new, there were two sisters. The oldest sister had no baby, but the younger sister did. The youngest sister never seemed to be able to get the housework and gardening all done, maybe because she rested so often.

She often had her older sister watch her baby girl, Nkauj Ncoom (pronounced "Kow Chong") for her. She would just stand outside the window and call her sister, even though everyone in the village understood they should be quiet so they wouldn't draw attention to the village. Then the young mother would pass her baby through the window to the older sister. While her older sister had the baby, the mother would clean house, cook, or sometimes just take a nap.

One evening, she called out to her sister and passed the baby through the window. But it wasn't her sister in the house. It was a large female tiger. The tiger took Nkauj Ncoom and ran out of the village with the baby in her paws. Just on the edge of the village, the tiger took the baby's clothes off. She killed a dog and smeared the baby's clothes with blood. Then the tiger took the dog's carcass with her and left the baby's clothes to trick the villagers. She ran off to the jungle with the baby.

When the young mother finished her work, she called to get the baby back, but after she had called several times, her sister kept repeating that she did not have the baby. She had not seen it at all that evening. The mother went into her sister's house and said, "I don't believe you. I've come to see for myself." She looked everywhere in her sister's house, but there was no baby. They discussed what might have happened. "It was all my fault," moaned the mother. "I should not have done that. I was just too lazy, always calling to you and leaving the baby." They became alarmed and started to search.

Eventually they found the bloody baby clothes and feared a roaming tiger had snatched and killed the baby.

Meanwhile, the mother tiger gently carried the baby to a cave in the mountains and raised the child as her own. When the little girl reached puberty, the mother tiger asked her if she wanted to learn to make *pa ndau*.

"Yes," the girl said, "but we live in the jungle. Who will teach me to sew? Where will we get the material to do it? We don't have silver coins or anything."

That night the tiger lurked along the trail used by the Chinese merchants. The tiger surprised a pair of merchants, who dropped everything and ran away in terror. The tiger then gathered what she needed—fabric, coins, thread, and needles.

The next night the tiger went to a village to find which woman was the most skillful with needlework. In the morning she waited along the path for the woman to go to work in the fields. When the woman got close to her, the tiger jumped in front of her. The poor woman fainted and the tiger picked her up and carried her off to the cave.

There, the woman discovered she was not in danger if she just taught Nkauj Ncoom how to make *pa ndau*. After the woman had taught the girl everything, the tiger blindfolded the woman and took her back to her village. The tiger made the woman promise not to tell where she had been and what she had seen and done. It was easy for the woman to give her promise because the tiger told the woman that she would come back and kill her otherwise.

When it was time for the New Year's festival the tiger asked the girl if she wanted to go to the celebration. "Oh, yes," said the girl.

So the girl made clothes specially for the festival, just as the woman had taught her to do. (It is believed that you must have new clothes for the new year if you want to have good luck.) She was finished sewing just in time for the festival.

The tiger carried the girl to the park at the edge of the village. The girl ran to join the young people at the festival. She joined the lines of boys and girls tossing balls back and forth to each other. That evening the tiger waited for the girl to come so she could carry her back to the cave.

On the next day of the festival the tiger again carried the girl to the edge of the village. Again, the girl joined the young people playing ball. As she played, she sang, "The hoe is very sharp, and I'm living with a ghost tiger."

One of the village girls heard her song and came up to her and asked her, "Where do you live?"

"I live in the jungle," the girl told her.

The village girl smiled at her and said, "Will you be coming back tomorrow? There will be dances and more games."

"Oh, yes, I will be back again," was the answer. Again, in the evening, the tiger's daughter ran to the edge of the park and disappeared.

That night the local girl told her family, "Today I met a stranger who looked enough like me to be a sister."

Her mother, who was really the mother of the lost daughter, asked her to bring the girl home to lunch the next day. "It is important that you bring her home so we can talk with her. Get her here however you can," the mother said.

The next day, they invited the girl home for lunch. She didn't want to go, so her new friends, really her sister and sisters-in-law, had to push and pull her to their home. When they got to the house the mother asked, "Dear little girl, where do you live? Who do you live with? Who is your mother? Is she Hmong, Laotian, or Chinese?"

"I live in the jungle with a big tiger for a mother," said Nkauj Ncoom.

When the mother heard that the girl lived in the jungle with a tiger she knew that this girl must be her missing baby. She told the girl the story of how her own baby girl had disappeared.

"Come live with us," said the sister and sisters-in-law.

"No, I cannot. The tiger will find us and kill us all. My mother is a very powerful tiger," replied the girl.

And so they planned what they would do. "Don't be afraid. When you get back to the cave tonight, tell your mother that you have eaten all kinds of meats except elephant and wooly mammoth. Tell her you want to eat them, too."

That night, back at the cave with the tiger, Nkauj Ncoom did what they had planned. "I have eaten all the meats of the world except elephant and wooly mammoth, Mother. Why can't I have some of these meats, too?" asked the girl.

"Of course, my dear," agreed the tiger. "I will do anything for you."

The tiger blocked the cave entrance with a rock the next morning and left to get the meat. She traveled far away and finally found an elephant. The tiger had to jump on the elephant to bite it on the head. Naturally the elephant attacked her, and the tiger fell. This went on many times until the tiger finally killed the elephant. She carried the meat back to the cave.

As she neared the cave, the tiger called, "My dear Nkauj Ncoom, are you still home?"

"Yes, Mother," came the answer.

After they ate a feast of elephant meat, Nkauj Ncoom said, "That was different. Now the only meat in the world I have never eaten is wooly mammoth meat. Why can't I have some of it?"

The tiger left again and this time she was gone for one month. During that time the girl's family came and took Nkauj Ncoom back to their village to live with them.

When the tiger returned with the meat of the wooly mammoth, she called out, "My dear Nkauj Ncoom, are you still home?" There was no answer, so she called again, louder. "My dear, sweet Nkauj Ncoom, are you still home?" The cave was empty, and she could see that Nkauj Ncoom had been gone for a long time. The tiger started to search for her, but it was fall and the trail was covered with leaves. The tiger couldn't find Nkauj Ncoom's trail, so the mother tiger went into the cave, and there she sits and cries.

# *T*he Orphan and the Monkeys

housands of years ago, there was an orphan who lived with his elder brother and sister-in-law. His sister-in-law did not like him. In fact, she planned to kill him. The orphan was very sad and cried because he was so lonely.

His sister-in-law gave him dried seeds to plant, and everyone knows that dried seeds are no good for growing things. But he sowed all of the seeds in the field. Of course, many of them did not grow, but surprisingly, some of the seeds did sprout.

As the plants in his garden grew and the grain ripened, the monkeys kept stealing his corn and rice. The orphan decided to ask the shoa, or wise man, for help.

"Why do the monkeys keep coming to take all of my corn?" the orphan asked the shoa. "I can't make them stay away. I am a poor man and I need all the crops I can grow."

"Go home, kill a chicken, cook it, and eat some of it. Put some of what is left in your nose, your eyes, and your ears. Then go to the path made by the monkeys and go to sleep in the middle of it," counseled the wise man.

The orphan did as he was told. He killed a chicken, boiled it in water, and ate some of it. Afterwards he put some of the chicken in his eyes, his ears, and his nose. He found the monkeys' trail and laid down in the middle of it and went to sleep.

The monkeys found him on the trail and thought he was dead. "Who died here?" they asked. They picked up the orphan and carried him to the mountains where they lived. The monkeys had a big funeral ceremony for the dead farmer and invited many animals to come and join them. All the animals that came brought gold and money to put around the orphan as he lay on the blanket.

Suddenly the farmer sat up and lunged at the animals, yelling "Yah-h-h-h!" as loudly as he could. All of the shocked and frightened animals ran away. The monkeys ran up into the trees.

Then the orphan calmly picked up all the gold and silver and went home a rich man. When he got to the home of his brother and sister-in-law and showed them the fortune, they asked him, "Where did you get all of those riches?"

He told them the story of the monkeys and how he had tricked them. And so, the orphan lived with his family and shared his wealth with them. He was never sad or lonely again.

# The Orphan Boy and His Wife

A long time ago, an old woman said to an orphan, "I'm sorry your mother and father are dead. You need a wife."

The orphan boy said, "I can't marry anyone. I don't have any clothes. I don't have a house. I don't have any money."

The old woman said, "You can marry a wife. Go sit by the road and watch. All kinds of people will come by. Some will be dressed very elegantly and look very nice. You should not bother with those people. When you see three sisters riding on thin, sickly, dirty horses with dry manure all over them, the one you want is the youngest sister, who will be riding on the last horse. Speak to the three sisters. You should grab the tail of the youngest sister's horse and never let go of it no matter what happens."

So the orphan sat by the road and watched. There were many people coming by on the road. Some were dressed in silk and silvery clothes and were very attractive. Then he saw three sisters riding dirty horses. He grabbed the last horse's tail and held on to it. Nia Ngao Zhua Pa looked at him and said, "Please let go of my horse's tail. I am in a hurry."

He didn't do as she asked. Her oldest sister said, "Nia Ngao Zhua Pa, why argue with this orphan? He may be the husband fortune sent to you."

Nia Ngao Zhua Pa tried to ruffle herself up to scare him, like a hen does with her feathers. He just said, "Oh, that doesn't scare me a bit."

After a while she went with him and she married him. First, Nia Ngao Zhua Pa took some leaves and changed them into a beautiful house. Then she took off her ring and changed it into a rice pot. Then she took off her bracelet and changed it into a stove. She took half a grain of rice. He thought it was too little. "How can it be enough for both of us to eat?" he asked.

"Don't worry," she said. "There will be plenty. If there is not enough, you may eat it all and I won't have any."

She changed it into a pot full of rice. Then she took a flower and changed it into a cooked chicken. The orphan was surprised and knew he had a good wife. He was happy and rich.

But after a long time of watching their happiness, a neighbor girl, Nia Ngao Kou Kaw, said, "The orphan and his wife are rich. I'm poor. I want to be rich, too."

She was jealous. She thought, "I will hurt the orphan's wife." Then she said to the orphan, "Your wife is a bad woman. She drank dragon's blood. She drank nine bowls of dragon's blood. Tell your wife to go away and I will marry you. I will be a good wife."

For three days the neighbor girl Nia Ngao Kou Kaw said to the orphan, "Your wife is a bad woman. I am beautiful. Tell your wife to go away. I will marry you."

So the orphan said to his wife, Nia Ngao Zhua Pa, "A beautiful young girl wants to marry me." Many days of this went on, and finally one day he told his wife to go away, but his wife didn't want to go away. She said, "I want to live with you." The orphan began to tell her regularly to go away.

"I want to marry a beautiful young girl. I don't want you here." So the orphan's wife went to the lake. She walked into it. She said, "Please, my husband, tell me to come back."

But the husband didn't say anything. The wife said, "Please, my husband. The water is up to my knees. Tell me to come back."

But the husband didn't say anything. The wife said, "Please, my husband. The water is up to my waist. Tell me to come back."

But the husband didn't say anything. The wife implored him, "Please, my husband. The water is up to my neck. Tell me to come back."

But the husband still didn't say anything. And then the water was over his wife's head. She was gone. The orphan went home, but his house was gone, and only leaves were in its place. He said, "Where is my beautiful house?" He married the neighbor girl, Nia Ngao Kou Kaw, but he was not happy. He took to regularly visiting the lake where his wife was. He sat down by the lake and he cried, "I want to see Nia Ngao Zhua Pa."

A frog that happened to be nearby heard him and said, "I can drink the water. I can drink all the water. Then you can see Nia Ngao Zhua Pa. But, don't laugh! You must not laugh."

So the frog drank and drank. He drank half the water and his stomach got very big. The orphan laughed, "Ha, ha, ha!" and the frog's stomach burst open, *poosh*!

The water went back into the lake—*swoosh*! The orphan looked at the lake. He said, "What can I do? I want to see Nia Ngao Zhua Pa. I want to tell her to come back! Who can help me? I know, I'll go to the shoa. He knows everything. He will tell me what to do." And so the orphan went to see the shoa.

The shoa gave him advice. "Go and beg the frog again. Sew his stomach back up."

The orphan did as he was instructed. He begged the frog to try again. The frog finally agreed. "Remember, you must not laugh. If you do I'll never do it again for you." So the orphan promised and sewed the frog's stomach back up. The frog drank and drank the water again, and this time the orphan didn't laugh.

When the water was gone he saw his wife at the bottom of the lake, making needlework, sewing beautiful *pa ndau*. He looked back at the frog, who looked ridiculous, and, forgetting his promise, he laughed. This time the frog was furious. "If you were really sad you wouldn't laugh at me no matter how silly I look. I am not going to help you again."

The orphan cried and cried and begged the frog, but the frog refused to drink the water. The orphan sadly dragged himself home. The next day he came back to the lake. He sat on the shore and cried, and cried, and cried. The frog wandered by and heard him crying.

The orphan saw the frog and started to beg him to drink the water. He begged, pleaded, and cried. The frog felt sorry for the orphan, so he drank the water again and this time the orphan didn't laugh. After a while he saw his wife at the bottom of the lake, and he jumped in with her. He grabbed her by the arm and spoke to her.

"You wanted to marry a young girl," she reminded him. "You have a black heart and are very bad. Why are you still following me?"

The orphan begged her to forgive him. He told her, "I had been tempted so many times I became weak. I am sorry. Please, please, please forgive me."

Finally she relented, and today they are living at the bottom of the lake—married forever.

# The Tigers Steal Nou Plai's Wife, Ntxawm

A long time ago, Ntxawm told her husband, Nou Plai, "I would like to visit my parents for a short time." Since the fields wouldn't need her attention for a while, Nou Plai agreed. He walked with Ntxawm for quite a way, playing his *keng* (bamboo instrument) as he went. When they had traveled awhile and were near Ntxawm's family village, they thought they heard Ntxawm's family out collecting firewood. Ntxawm said, "I think my parents are collecting firewood near here. You can return home now." With that, he turned and went back home.

Ntxawm continued on, following the sounds, and then came to a clearing in the forest where she thought her family would be. But instead she saw many tigers coming toward her. Frightened, she called out loud, "Nou Plai, it's not my parents! It is huge tigers!" But Nou Plai was playing his *keng* and couldn't hear her well.

He replied, "You say to play it louder?" He continued to play his *keng* even louder. Ntxawm called again, but it didn't do any good.

She tried to get away from the tigers, but she could not. One small tiger came to Ntxawm and offered her his back to ride on, but she refused him. A larger tiger came to her and did the same thing, but she also refused him. The largest tiger was the third one to offer Ntxawm a ride on his back. Again she refused. Then the huge tiger frightened her by showing his giant white teeth, so Ntxawm agreed. She climbed onto the back of the giant tiger and he carried her away to a cave in a faraway jungle.

Many days after this, Nou Plai traveled to Ntxawm's parents' home. It was time for her to come back to their home after her visit. When he got to her parents' home he did not see her. "Where is Ntxawm?" he asked.

The reply surprised him. "She never was here."

"Ntxawm came here a long time ago. I walked with her myself until we heard you gathering firewood and I went back," stated Nou Plai. Ntxawm's parents became suspicious and thought that he might have killed her. They became very angry. They finally demanded payment from Nou Plai for the loss of their daughter. They asked for so much payment that he became very poor.

Frantically Nou Plai searched everywhere for Ntxawm. He found the tracks of the tigers and trailed them. After a long time Nou Plai came to a clump of bamboo. Since he was weary, he crawled under the clump and slept. While he slept, Ntxawm and the tigers passed nearby in the forest. She was surprised when they accidentally found Nou Plai sleeping. The tigers wanted to eat him. Ntxawm quickly told the tigers, "Don't kill him. He is my brother." She tried to wake him up but he was sleeping so soundly he didn't wake.

The tigers granted her wish not to eat Nou Plai, and the tigers and Ntxawm started walking in the jungle. She lied to the tigers, "I have lost my comb. I'll just hurry back and find it." She went back to the sleeping Nou Plai and tried to wake him again but had no luck. She put her comb and leaves and flowers on him and went back to the tigers.

They walked farther for a while and then she lied to the tigers again. "I have lost my bracelet. I'll hurry back and find it." She went back to the sleeping Nou Plai and again tried to waken him. She grabbed his body and shook him with no luck. She left her bracelet on him with the comb, leaves, and flowers and went back to the tigers.

When she got back to the tigers they continued walking, getting farther away. But her heart could not leave Nou Plai behind, so she lied again. "Oh, goodness! I seem to have lost my ring. Don't worry, I'll hurry back and find it." When she got to the sleeping Nou Plai she slapped his face and called to him but he never woke up. "Nou Plai, maybe we weren't meant to be husband and wife," she cried and left her ring. She went back to the tigers brokenhearted and defeated.

Together Ntxawm and the tigers traveled for many days. They decided to take Ntxawm far away to a very remote place where she would not have a chance to escape. Whenever they stopped to sleep they built an open fire.

Meanwhile, after a long sleep, Nou Plai woke up. He had slept so long that vines had grown and tied his body. The comb had sprouted and become a tree—it already had fruit and birds in the tree eating the fruit. In fact, some fruit dropped on him and that was what woke him up.

The sword by his side had rusted. It took him a long time to break loose from the vines. He found the ring and bracelet that Ntxawm had placed on his chest and realized that he had slept a long, long time. Nou Plai started to look for Ntxawm again. He tracked the tigers and found firepits where the rain had washed away the ashes until the pits were almost gone.

As he traveled, the firepits became fresher and fresher. When he found no more pits, he knew that he was close to the tigers and Ntxawm. He sharpened his sword and took a tender banana leaf. He blew on the leaf and the floating message whispered, "Where did the tiger carry my Ntxawm? Where are you? If you hear me, answer." He blew on it three times, but there was no answer. He traveled to the other side of the mountain and blew on the leaf again. "Where are you? Where did the tiger carry you? If you hear me, answer." But there was no answer.

He traveled in another direction near the mountain and stopped to blow on the leaf again. "Where are you, my dear Ntxawm? Where did the tiger carry you? If you hear me, answer."

This time, Ntxawm was in a cave in the mountain and she heard him. She blew on a leaf and whispered, "The tiger has carried me to the cave in the mountain."

Ntxawm heard his response. "Can I come to the cave?"

"No," she advised, "because the tigers are huge. They will eat you. Go back. It is too late now."

Nou Plai kept looking for the cave. He finally found it and looked through a hole in the top of the cave. He saw Ntxawm below in the cave, sewing. He leaned over the hole and spat on her. She didn't look up at the roof of the cave as she said, "The sun is shining but there is rain dropping on my *pa ndau*." Nou Plai cut a branch and dropped it to her. She grabbed the branch and smelled the fresh cut of the wood from his sword. She looked up this time.

"Can I come down?" Nou Plai asked.

"You must wait. I must check to see if it is safe first." Ntxawm put some water in a bowl and put it at the opening of the cave and looked through it. She saw the tigers returning. "Don't come now," she cautioned. "They are returning."

"When can I come?" he whispered.

"If you really want, you can come briefly after they are asleep. Go away now. They'll smell you," she warned.

The tigers came after Nou Plai had gone. Ntxawm's tiger mother-in-law said, "Daughter-in-law, why did you stay home today? You smell like fresh rice."

"Don't say that, mother-in-law," said Ntxawm. "You eat with your mouth and now you smell what you ate with your nose. I don't have anything."

The tiger father-in-law came in and asked Ntxawm, "Daughter-in-law, why did you stay home today? You smell like fresh rice."

"Don't say that, father-in-law," repeated Ntxawm. "You eat with your mouth and now you smell what you ate with your nose. I don't have anything."

One by one her older brothers-in-law, their wives, her younger brothers-in-law, and their wives came in and they all said the same thing. They all got the same answer. Then her tiger husband came in. "Ntxawm, why did you stay home today? You smell like fresh rice." He, too, got the same response.

They had brought back a deer and a boar and a Laotian woman they had killed. They had them for dinner. Then they all fell asleep. Ntxawm went to the opening of the cave, where she met Nou Plai.

"Let's run away," said Nou Plai.

"No, we can't, because the tigers will come after us," cautioned Ntxawm.

"I will kill the tigers," promised Nou Plai.

"You can't kill them all. They are too strong and big," she said. They talked for a while and then Ntxawm said, "There will be other times when the tigers will sleep deeply. It will be safer then."

"When is the best time?" he asked.

"Go and look at the tree at the top of the cave. When the leaves turn yellow and start to fall, that will be the time," she answered.

He waited and watched. When the leaves turned yellow and started to fall, Nou Plai came back. He killed the tigers and when he was about to kill Ntxawm's tiger husband she stopped him. "No. I have stayed with him a long time. Spare him," she said. "I am pregnant with his young."

"I cannot. I have come this far," and so Nou Plai killed the tiger.

Ntxawm went to another room in the cave and transformed into a tiger. She came out, menacing. Nou Plai raised his sword. "Are you playing games or are you serious?" he asked. "If you are serious, and if you are long I'll cut you into three pieces. If you are short I'll cut you into two pieces."

Ntxawm broke into tears. She changed back into human form, and they left the cave for the trip back to their home. About halfway, she told him, "Wait here." She went into a cave. "I will stay here a long time. Go watch the nearby tree. When the leaves of the tree are yellow don't come and look at me."

He waited and watched. The leaves of the tree changed from green to yellow, fell down, and the tree grew new leaves. Ntxawm stayed quietly in the cave. When the tree's leaves came back to green and turned yellow again, Nou Plai became impatient and went to look. He saw a pile of decay.

He was very sad and started to return home alone. As he walked, Ntxawm called to him. "Nou Plai. If you don't want me why did you kill all the tigers, bring me halfway home, and leave me alone? How will I survive?"

He came back and waited. Yellow leaves all fell again. Tiny green leaves grew, turned yellow and were ready to fall once more. He went to see Ntxawm again. Just as before, all he saw was a pile of decay.

"No matter what, this time I am going away!" he shouted. He walked away, and as he was leaving he heard Ntxawm call to him. "I don't care. She's just lying to me," he thought.

She called to him again. He decided to come back. He waited again and saw the leaves turn yellow and fall. Wearily, he looked in the cave again and there was a pile of decay. He was brokenhearted and decided that this time he would leave and forget about her. As he walked away, she called again, "Nou Plai. If you don't want me why did you kill all the tigers, bring me halfway home, and leave me alone? How will I survive?"

He pretended not to hear her call, because he thought that she just lied to him to get him to wait for her and that she would never come back anyway. But she continued to call him and finally he decided to give her one more chance. He returned to the cave and waited until the tiny little leaves began to form and grew big again. Then Ntxawm called him to come back and help her.

He went back to the cave. There, she had given birth to two tiger babies. Her tiger skin was beside her. Nou Plai raised his sword to kill the tiger babies but Ntxawm stopped him. "Are you going to take them with you?" he asked her.

They left the young tigers. Ntxawm asked him to bring her tiger skin to the valley and place it on the rock and say, "This is your possession. Come and get it." She told him not to look back.

Nou Plai did as she told him, but he looked back at the tiger skin and saw the tigers running to tear the skin apart. Nou Plai came back to Ntxawm and they finally went home.

When they got to the village of Nou Plai's parents, they discovered that Nou Plai's family was holding the ceremony that would release the soul of the dead so it could be reborn again. Nou Plai had been gone so long his parents had given him up for dead.

They knew that if they walked in during the ceremony Nou Plai's parents would be extremely shocked, so they went to stay in a rice storage building. When Nou Plai heard the *keng* playing the music that gave Nou Plai's name and the message to release his soul, he waited until it was over and the musician had put the *keng* away. He then picked up his own *keng* and played on it, "You released Nou Plai's soul but he is here. He has returned." He played this several times.

His father heard it and was stunned. "Is what I am hearing right?" he whispered. The father went to the *keng* player and recognized Nou Plai. He was filled with joy. "My son is alive—my son is alive—my son is really alive!"

Nou Plai's mother ran to the front door of the house from the kitchen where she had been. She ran so fast she hit her leg on something sharp and tore her leg. But that didn't stop her as she rushed to greet Nou Plai.

They stopped the ceremony then and began to celebrate Nou Plai's return. "Where is our daughter-in-law?" asked Nou Plai's parents.

"Waiting in the rice storage building," he replied.

They told him, "Bring her back to the house and we will all celebrate together." And they all did!

# Gwa and Uo and Their Two Fish Wives

A long time ago, there were two orphan boys named Gwa and Uo. They were all alone and quite poor. One day while they were going fishing, which they did every day, an old dragon man saw them and asked, "Are you two going to fish?"

They replied, "Yes. We are going to fish."

"If you will give me your fishing poles, I will try to see if I can catch two fish for you," offered the old dragon man.

Gwa and Uo gave him their fishing poles and, sure enough, he caught two fish for them. He warned them, "Take these two fish home, but you are not to cook them to eat. You should wash a jar and place them in there safely. Remember, do not eat them."

Gwa and Uo agreed, "Yes, we will do as you say and place them in a jar."

When they arrived home, Gwa, the oldest brother, was hungry and thought only of eating, so he quickly put his fish on the ashes in the fireplace. "Don't do that," Uo reminded him. "Don't you remember that the old dragon man said that we should not eat the fish but instead put them in a jar?"

"Oh, yes, I had forgotten," said Gwa, and he quickly pulled his fish out of the fireplace. The fish had been there long enough, however, for some of it to burn. They washed out a jar and placed the two fish in it.

Every day they worked on their farm. When they went out to work the day after they had put the fish in the jar, the two fish were transformed into two young ladies who cleaned the house neatly and prepared dinner for Gwa and Uo. This happened for many days. Gwa and Uo thought it was the neighbors who had come to clean and cook for them, so they went to thank the neighbors.

The neighbors denied having anything to do with it. In fact, some of the neighbors even scolded them. "You have your own people who do things for you. We have our own people to clean and cook for us. They are so busy they wouldn't have time to come and clean and cook for you, too."

The brothers decided to ask the shoa (the prophet) about the matter. "What can I do for you?" the shoa asked when they arrived at his place.

They explained, "Shoa, every day we leave our home to work on our farm and when we return home, our house is clean and dinner is prepared for us. We do not know who does this for us. We thought it was the neighbors, so we went to thank them and they told us they had not done it. Therefore, we come to you to ask if you can tell us who does all of these things for us."

The shoa answered, "It is just as some of your neighbors have told you. You have your own people who do things for you. It would be better to let things go on this way for a bit longer. Don't be in a hurry to find out and it will last longer. But if you cannot wait, then I will tell you all about it."

They said, "We can't wait any longer. We would like to see who does these things for us."

"If you insist," said the shoa. "In the morning pretend that you are going to go to the field. But before you do, hide the comb, the brush, and the sweeper. Then bring some ashes and pepper and climb very quietly and sit in the storage space in the attic. Stay there and wait. When the sun is

121

*Folk Stories of Love, Magic, and Fun*

turning home, you will see two ladies come out of your bedroom. They will look for the things you have hidden. When they climb up to look in the attic, scatter a little of your ashes and pepper at them and say, 'If you want to be human, you should become human. If you want to be spirits, you should remain as spirits. If you just keep transforming back and forth like you do, you only disturb people and they will laugh at you.' After you have said that, you should come down out of the attic."

Gwa and Uo went back home. The next morning they did just as the shoa had told them to do. They hid the comb, the brush, and the sweeper and took some ashes and pepper with them to the attic. They sat up there quietly.

When the sun was turning home, two beautiful young ladies giggled as they walked out of the bedroom. One of them began to look for the comb to comb her hair, but she could not find it. She remarked, "The comb was always here. How come it is not here today? I wonder where they put it."

The other lady looked for the sweeper to sweep the floor, but she could not find it. "The sweeper was always in here. Where did they put it?" she said.

The lady who was looking for the comb went to the kitchen to look for the brush to brush the rice steamer. But she could not find it either. She mumbled, "The brush is not in its place. Where did they put everything today?"

The second lady answered her, "Maybe they put everything in the attic. Let's go up there and look for them."

Both of them climbed up to the attic where Gwa and Uo were sitting. When the four of them saw each other Gwa and Uo scattered ashes and pepper at the two ladies. The brothers said, "If you want to be human, you should become human. If you want to be spirits, you should remain as spirits. But if you just keep transforming back and forth like you have been doing, you only disturb other people and they will laugh at you."

The two ladies rushed down and ran to the jar together but the jar only fit one of each lady's legs. Gwa and Uo ran quickly after them and pulled them back.

Since Gwa had put his fish in the fireplace and burned it a bit, his lady had some burn scars. But Uo had not burned his fish, so his lady was very pretty. Gwa decided he did not want to marry his lady with the burns, he wanted to marry Uo's lady. They kept arguing back and forth and back and forth.

Uo said, "Mine is the one without scars from burning."

Gwa answered him, "Mine is the one who has no scars."

After a long time of arguing, Uo seemed to be losing. It began to look like Gwa would get to marry Uo's pretty lady, so Uo's lady helped him. She said, "I belong to Uo because he did not burn his fish. She belongs to Gwa because he burned his fish in the fireplace."

After she said this, Gwa knew he had lost, so he married his lady, even though he really didn't want to. Uo married his beautiful lady. The two brothers built two houses and each couple lived in one house.

Each couple prepared a field to grow plants they could use to make fiber for clothes. When the plants were ready to be cut Uo's wife and Gwa's wife processed the fiber very differently. That was because Uo's wife hadn't been burned and she remembered her magic. She transformed into a pig and ate the fiber plants during the day. At night, she sat down by the

light of the lantern and just pulled shining silk fabric from her belly button.

Since Gwa's wife had been burned, she had forgotten her magic. So she did just as all other Hmong women did. She cut all the fiber plants, peeled the skins, and dried them in the sun. Then she would weave them into cloth. After that, she made the clothes from the cloth. Her fabric was not shining and soft like that of Uo's wife.

One day Uo went to Gwa's house and saw Gwa's wife weaving and asked, "How come your wife makes fabric like that? My wife does it very differently, and her fabrics are definitely better, too."

Gwa told Uo, "Everybody makes fabric the way my wife does. You say your wife has a better way of doing it—you must be lying, Uo!"

"I am not," said Uo. "If you don't believe me, come and see for yourself tonight."

Gwa replied, "I will have to see it to believe it." So after dinner, Gwa rode a pig to Uo's house to watch Uo's wife make fabric. But the pig made loud noises as they traveled to Uo's house, so Uo's wife knew someone was coming. She blew out the lamp and went to sleep. When Gwa arrived and looked through a hole, he saw that the house was very dark and Uo's wife was asleep.

The next day Uo went back to visit Gwa in his house and Gwa remarked, "Uo, you said your wife is very hard working. You are a liar. Last night when I went to your house she was already asleep. She cannot be compared to my hard-working wife."

Uo told him, "Who told you to ride a pig to our house? The pig made too much noise so when my wife heard the noise she quit working."

That night, Gwa decided to go to Uo's house again. This time he rode a cow, but it also made a lot of noise. Uo's wife heard the cow coming, so she again blew out the light and went to sleep. When Gwa got there, the house was as dark as the night before.

The next day Uo was at Gwa's house and Gwa snorted, "Uo, you said your wife is a hard-working woman. I have gone to your house two nights now and she was always asleep."

Uo laughed at Gwa. "Who told you to ride a cow? It made too many noises. When she heard all the noise, she blew out the light and went to sleep."

The third night Gwa rode a horse, and the same thing happened. He did not get to see her that night either. By now Gwa was sure that Uo was just lying about the whole thing, so he was not going to try again.

The local chieftain held a feast a few days later, and he invited both Gwa and Uo. The morning of the day of the feast they both set out for the chieftain's village. Gwa wore his new clothes that his wife had just made for him. Uo was dressed in his old clothes. Gwa said to Uo, "Uo, don't you have any new clothes to wear?"

"Yes, I have," replied Uo. "But this is good enough."

"If you don't have anything to wear better than that I will let you wear some of mine," offered Gwa. "They will be better than the ones you are wearing now."

"No, this is fine," said Uo.

The two of them set out for the feast. Gwa said, "Uo, if you don't change to better clothes, I am afraid that when we arrive the chieftain will not let you eat any food."

"Well, if that is the case then I will just return home," Uo stated.

"But you will lose face," argued Gwa.

"I don't care about that at all," was Uo's answer.

When they got close to the village, Uo said, "Gwa, wait here for me. I have to go urinate behind the bushes." Gwa agreed and Uo went to the bushes. Uo took out his fine silk clothes from his bag and put them on. His clothes were shining and elegant.

When Uo came out of the bushes Gwa thought Uo's clothes were the most beautiful things he had ever seen. Gwa felt bad now, thinking that his clothes were not as good as Uo's.

In the village, Uo was greeted by masses of people. Even the chieftain grabbed Uo's arm and invited Uo to sit by his side to eat. No food was given to Gwa—in fact, they wouldn't even let him into the house. Gwa was hungry, hurt, and angry. He returned home.

When the feast was over, Uo looked everywhere for Gwa but he couldn't find him. Uo walked home alone.

That night Gwa walked over to Uo's house to find out how Uo's wife made her cloth. Because he walked and didn't ride any animals, there was no noise and Uo's wife didn't know he was coming. She sat by the light of the lamp and pulled beautiful fabric from her belly button.

When Gwa saw this he went home and started to think of ways to kill Uo so that he could have Uo's amazing wife. The next day Gwa went to Uo's house and asked Uo to come cut down a tree with him. Uo, who was not very clever, agreed to go with him. But Uo's wife suspected something, so she called Uo into their bedroom, gave him a big shirt, and said, "Uo, when Gwa tells you to go down to see which direction the tree will fall, put this shirt in there and then run away as fast as you can so that you will not get killed."

Gwa and Uo went into the forest to cut a huge tree. Each of them cut from a side of the tree. When Gwa knew that the tree was ready to fall down he told Uo, "Go down there and see which direction the tree is going to fall."

Uo did just as his wife had told him to do, and the tree fell on Uo's big shirt. Gwa didn't know what had happened, so he was very happy and thought, "Now you are dead. I can have your wife!"

When Gwa got home, there, to his surprise, was Uo, sitting on Gwa's front porch weaving a basket.

The next day Gwa went to Uo's house and asked Uo, "Would you please come with me to help me make a wooden rice pounder?" Uo agreed to go with Gwa again.

Uo's wife knew that Gwa wanted to kill Uo because he liked her very much and that he would do anything to kill Uo. This time she gave Uo a shirt with long sleeves to wear and told him what he should do.

Gwa and Uo built a wooden rice pounder that day, and when they had finished installing it Gwa said, "Uo, go and fix the bowl and let me see if it is going to work."

Uo put his long sleeves into the bowl. Gwa dropped the heavy pounding stick down and it hit Uo's long sleeves. Gwa thought the sleeves were Uo's hands. Uo pretended to be dead. Gwa was very happy and said, "Now you are really dead. I will take your wife."

Gwa returned home, but a bit later, Uo returned home, too.

The next day Gwa asked Uo to go with him to build a house over their parents' graves. This time Uo's wife could not help Uo anymore. The two brothers went and built a house to cover their parents' graves. Gwa said to Uo, "Go inside and tell me where light comes through so I will know where to cover the holes with wood." Because Uo was not very clever, he did as his brother asked. He went inside the house and pointed out every place where light was coming through.

Gwa put more wood on each spot and asked, "Where else?"

"There are holes on this side of the wall," said Uo. Gwa put more wood over the spots. They continued to work like this until the house was totally dark inside. Uo said, "There is no light coming through anymore. Open the door so I can come out."

Gwa did not open it. In fact, he sealed off the door even more tightly so that Uo couldn't break it. Gwa left Uo in the house and went home.

Uo's wife waited and waited, but Uo never came home. The next day Gwa sent his little daughter to ask Uo's wife to come stay with them. Uo's wife said, "Yes, I'll come, but first I need to kill a chicken to eat. Then I'll come." She killed the chicken.

The next day Gwa's daughter came back. "Come now and stay with us."

"Go tell your father I will come after I kill my pig. After I eat some pig I will come and stay with you," the wife said. She killed the pig, cooked it, and ate some of it.

The third day the little girl came back and said, "Come now and stay with us."

"Go tell your father I will come after I kill my cow. After I eat some cow meat I will come and stay with you," the wife said. She killed the cow, cooked it, and ate some of it. Through all of this Uo's wife wore the same clothes, and she wiped her greasy hands on her clothes until they were all quite slippery.

For a fourth time the little girl came and said, "Come now and stay with us."

"I'll come," answered the wife, "but tell your father he has to take me to see where he put my husband first."

The little girl went back to her father with this message. The next day Gwa came and took Uo's wife to where Uo was. "Open it. I want to see," she demanded.

He opened the house a little bit. "Open it more. It's not enough," she said, and he did.

"Open it more until it is big enough for me to get in," she demanded. He did. Uo's wife saw that Uo was dead and his body was already decaying. She jumped in the house. Since her clothes were so greasy and slippery, Gwa couldn't hold her when he tried to grab her. Gwa tore the house apart, but he didn't see anything. He dug down in the ground to his parents' graves. When he opened the coffins he saw only two rocks. He separated the two rocks, placing one on each side of the river.

Later Gwa returned and saw that the two rocks had become two trees. The trees arched over the river until they were joined at the top. Gwa became enraged with jealousy. "They must be Uo and his wife!" With that, he cut the trees down with his axe. He cut cord wood out of the trees and burned it all after the wood was dry. When he was done he didn't see anything on the ground. But when he looked up into the sky he saw two beautiful butterflies flying all the way up to the sky. "That must be them!" he roared.

Some time after that, Gwa's wife went to the river to get some water and she saw that a white pigeon had dropped a little white feather on the other side of the river. She got the feather and brushed one of her burn scars with it. The scar disappeared. She did the same thing all over her body wherever there was a scar, but there was one little spot behind her neck that she couldn't reach. She took the feather home and asked Gwa to brush that spot for her.

A pigeon flew to the top of the roof and landed there. It started to coo. The coos said, "Gwa is going to kill his wife. Gwa is going to kill his wife." Gwa heard, but he didn't pay any attention to it. He took the feather and brushed the little spot on the back of his wife's neck. With that, she died.

Then, just Gwa and his daughter remained.

*Tas*
(The End)

*Folk Stories of Love, Magic, and Fun*

# Bibliography

Adams, Nina S., and Alfred W. McCoy, eds. *Laos: War and Revolution.* New York: Harper and Row, 1970.

Bernatzik, Hugo Adolf. *Akha and Miao: Problems of Applied Ethnography in Farther India.* Translated from German by Nagler Alois. New Haven, Conn.: Human Relations Areas Files Press, 1970.

Campbell, Margaret, Nakorn Pongoi, and Chusak Voraphitak. *From the Hands of the Hills.* Hong Kong: Media Transasia Ltd., 1978.

Chaturabhand, Preecha. *Peoples of the Hills.* Bangkok, Thailand: Editions Duang Kamol, 1980.

"A Clan against All Odds." *Insight.* January 16, 1989.

Diamond, Norma. "The Miao and Poison: Interactions on China's Frontier." *Ethnology.* Vol. XXVII, 1988: 1-25.

Dykstra, Anne H. *Flower Cloth of the Hmong.* Denver, Colo.: Denver Museum of Natural History, 1985.

Everyingham, J. "One Family's Odyssey to America." *National Geographic.* Vol. 157, no. 5. May 1980.

Fairservis, Walter A., Jr. *Costume of the East.* Denver, Colo.: Denver Museum of Natural History, 1971.

"Fighting Tribe." *Time.* July 7, 1961: 21-22.

Garrett, W. E. "No Place to Run: The Hmong of Laos." *National Geographic.* Vol. 145, no. 1. January 1974.

_____. "Thailand, Refuge from Terror." *National Geographic.* Vol. 157, no. 5. May 1980.

Hamilton-Merritt, Jane. *Hmong and Yao: Mountain Peoples of Southeast Asia.* 1982. Survive, P.O. Box 50, Redding Ridge, CT 06876.

Hassel, Carla J. *Creating Pa Ndau Appliqué.* Lombard, Ill.: Wallace-Homestead Book Company, 1984.

Hendricks, Glenn I., Bruce T. Downing, and Amos S. Deinard. *The Hmong in Transition.* Staten Island, N.Y.: Center for Migration Studies of New York, Inc., 1986.

Herold, Joyce. *Flower Cloth of the Hmong.* Denver, Colo.: Denver Museum of Natural History, 1985.

*The Hill Tribes of Thailand.* Technical Service Club Tribal Research Institute, 1986.

How-Man, Wong. "Peoples of China's Far Provinces." *National Geographic.* Vol. 135, no. 3. March 1984.

Johnson, Charles. *Myths, Legends and Folk Tales from the Hmong of Laos.* St. Paul, Minn.: Macalester College, 1985.

_____. *Shoa and His Fire.* St. Paul, Minn.: Macalester College, 1981.

Johnson, Charles, ed. *The Monkeys and the Grasshoppers.* St. Paul, Minn.: Macalester College, 1981.

Laufer, Berthold. "The Myth of P'an-Hu, the Bamboo King." *Journal of American Folklore,* 30. 1917: 419-421.

Lemoine, J., and C. Mougne. "Why Has Death Stalked the Refugees?" *Natural History.* Vol. 92. November 1983: 6-19.

Lewis, Paul, and Elaine Lewis. *Peoples of the Golden Triangle.* London: Thames and Hudson Ltd., 1984.

McDowell, Bart. "Thailand: Luck of a Land in the Middle." *National Geographic.* Vol. 162, no. 4. October 1982.

Marshall, Elliot. "The Hmong: Dying of Culture Shock?" *Science*, 212. 1981: 1008.

Morin, Stephen. "Troubled Refugees: Many Hmong Puzzled by Life in U.S., Yearn for Old Days in Laos." *Wall Street Journal*. February 16, 1983: 1, 25.

Mottin, Jean. *History of the Hmong*. Bangkok, Thailand: Odeon Store Ltd., 1980.

Olney, Douglas. *The Hmong and Their Neighbors*. CURA Reporter, University of Minnesota, Center for Urban and Regional Affairs. Vol. 8, no. 1. 1983: 8-14.

Peterson, Sally. "Translating Experience and the Reading of a Story Cloth." *Journal of American Folklore*. Vol. 101, no. 399. January/March 1988: 6-22.

Pulleyblank, E. G. "The Chinese and Their Neighbors in Prehistoric and Early Historic Times." *The Origins of Chinese Civilization*. Berkeley, Calif.: University of California Press, 1983.

Quincy, Keith. *Hmong: History of a People*. Cheney, Wash.: Eastern Washington University Press, 1988.

Ranard, Donald A. "The Last Bus." *Atlantic Monthly*. October 1987: 26-34.

Randall, Joan, ed. *Art of the Hmong-Americans*. Davis, Calif.: University of California Press, 1985.

Schafer, Edward H. et al. *Ancient China*. New York: Time-Life Books, 1967.

Sherman, Spencer. "The Hmong in America." *National Geographic*. Vol. 174, no. 4. October 1988.

Snow, L. "Folk Medical Beliefs and Their Implications for Care of Patients." *Annals of Internal Medicine*. Vol. 81. 1974: 82-96.

Sochurek, Howard. "Viet Nam's Montagnards." *National Geographic*. Vol. 133, no. 4. April 1968.

Social Security Administration, Office of Refugee Resettlement. "The Hmong Resettlement Study." Prepared by Literacy and Language Program, Northwest Regional Educational Laboratory, Portland, Oregon, 1984.

Vreeland, Susan. "Future of Laotian Folk Art Hangs by a Thread." *Christian Science Monitor.* November 19, 1981: 15.

_____. "Through the Looking Glass with the Hmong of Laos." *Christian Science Monitor.* March 30, 1981: B13.

White, Peter. "Laos." *National Geographic.* Vol. 171, no. 6. June 1987.

_____. "Mosaic of Cultures." *National Geographic.* Vol. 139, no. 3. March 1971.

White, Virginia. *Pa Ndau: The Needlework of the Hmong.* Washington, D.C.: Cheney Free Press, 1982.

Willcox, Donald. *Hmong Folklife.* Penland, N.C.: Hmong Natural Association of North Carolina, 1986. (For information about this book, write Don Willcox, P.O. Box 1, Penland, NC 28765.)

## Video Productions

Livo, Norma J. *Hmong at Peace and War.* Sponsored by the Colorado Endowment for the Arts and Humanities and the University of Colorado at Denver, 1989. 15 minutes.

Livo, Norma J. *Hmong Folklore.* Sponsored by Colorado Endowment for the Arts and Humanities and the University of Colorado at Denver, 1989. 15 minutes.

Livo, Norma J. *Hmong Folkstories.* Sponsored by Colorado Endowment for the Arts and Humanities and the University of Colorado at Denver, 1989. 30 minutes.

---

The video productions above are also available in slide/tape format.

# About the Authors

Norma J. Livo received her B.S., M.Ed., and Ed.D. from the University of Pittsburgh, Pennsylvania. She has taught at the elementary and secondary levels and has been a professor of education at the University of Colorado at Denver since 1968. She is the mother of four children and the grandmother of five. Stories and storytelling are important to her in both her professional and personal life.

Dia Cha is a Hmong immigrant originally from Laos. She and some of her family escaped Laos shortly after the Vietnam War ended and have been in the United States for twelve years. She received her B.A. in anthropology from Metropolitan State College in Denver in 1989 and is currently working on an M.A. in anthropology from Northern Arizona University in Flagstaff.